No Lex 10-12

War Chief of the Seminoles

WAR CHIEF OF THE SEMINOLES

by MAY McNEER

Illustrated by LYND WARD

THIS SPECIAL EDITION IS PRINTED AND DISTRIBUTED BY ARRANGEMENT WITH THE ORIGINATORS AND PUBLISHERS OF LANDMARK BOOKS *Random House, Inc.*, NEW YORK, BY

E. M. HALE AND COMPANY

EAU CLAIRE, WISCONSIN

Fifth Printing

Published in New York by Random House, Inc.
and simultaneously in Toronto, Canada, by
Random House of Canada Ltd.

L. C. Catalog Card No.: 54-6271
Manufactured in the U.S.A.

To my cousin, Mary Weedon Keen,
who has also had a lifelong interest in Osceola

Contents

Foreword

Threads leading back to Osceola and the Seminole War have always been in my family pattern—important to me, to my brother, Weedon McNeer, and to my cousins. We grew up in the sands and the sun, the palmettos and the swamps, of Osceola's homeland. Our great-grandfather was Dr. Frederick Weedon of St. Augustine. He was mayor of that old, exciting little city in the year that Osceola killed General Wiley Thompson. And Wiley Thompson, whose death began the seven-year war, was my great-grandmother's brother.

Dr. Weedon had been a colonel and a surgeon in the army of Andrew Jackson when he fought the British and the Creek Indians. Great-grandfather planted one of the first big orange groves in Florida, and worked it with 350 slaves. His son-in-law was Dr. Daniel Whitehurst, who fought the Seminoles with the Florida militia and helped take King Philip. Yet Dr. Weedon stayed with Osceola from his capture to his death and was, Osceola said just before he died, his only white friend.

My family still owns Osceola's peace pipe, a silver neck ornament, a braided lock of his hair, and letters about the Seminole war leader. I have wanted to write a book about Osceola ever since I can remember. Doing so has been a real satisfaction.

MAY McNEER

War Chief of the Seminoles

1

Who Is That Indian?

One day in 1823, the white man's army was lined up for drill at Fort Brooke in Florida.

"Attention!–Shoulder arms–Right face–Forward march!"

Back and forth, wheeling up and down in good formation, the men sweated in hot blue uniforms as their boots kicked up soft white sand. They were drilling in front of a log stockade that had been recently built on the spur of land where the Hillsborough River flowed into Tampa Bay. Gulls circled overhead, dipping and turning. A lone pelican dived lazily for a fish every now and then in the warm water.

"Column–left!"

Leaning against a gnarled old live oak tree, where gray moss trailed over his head, was an Indian youth of about eighteen or nineteen. He stood there, against the tree trunk, silent and motionless, watching intently every step of the marching troops.

The Indian youth watched the marching troops intently

"Company halt!—Left face—Order arms—Company dismissed!"

When the soldiers had broken ranks and walked off, calling comments to one another about the heat and mosquitoes, a young lieutenant asked a captain curiously, "Who is that Indian? Other Seminoles come and go, and they all seem alike to me, but that one looks different. He acts differently too."

The captain glanced at the Indian. "His name is Osceola. I tried to talk to him last week when he watched us, but he can't speak English. Louis says he's from a village on Peace Creek, south of here."

The captain hailed an old Negro who was walking past the log fort.

"Hey, Louis, come here a minute!"

As the old man approached, the captain called, "Louis, ask that Indian why he watches the troops so often."

Louis had been a slave belonging to a Spanish family. His master had given him his freedom, and now he was working as an interpreter at the fort. He could speak English, Spanish, and both of the Seminole dialects. As he addressed the young Seminole, the captain and the lieutenant strolled over to listen, although they understood none of the conversation.

The old man was speaking in Mickasukee to the Indian, and the young warrior listened quietly. Then a smile broke over his face. His eyes looked intelligent as well as proud, but his smile was so friendly and warm that the two white men took an instant liking to him.

"What did he say, Louis?" asked the captain.

"Sir, he says that he likes to watch the soldiers march, and he likes to see the soldiers fire their guns. I ask, would he like a gun some day, and he says, yes, he would like that very much."

"Peace Creek is quite a distance from here," said the captain. "Does he come back and forth often?"

Louis smiled. "This boy, sir, he comes often and it is no trouble to him to come that far. He is the fastest runner of all the Seminoles. He's a Mickasukee—a Red Stick—and the Mickasukees are the best hunters, the best runners, and the best fighters, too."

The lieutenant looked confused. He was fresh from West Point Military Academy, and a native of Virginia. He didn't know much about the Indians down here in Florida.

"I thought he was a Seminole," said the lieutenant.

The captain was from Georgia, where the Seminoles had lived before coming to Florida some years before. He knew the Indians quite well.

"The Seminoles are made up of bands from several tribes," he said. "Seminole means 'separatist' or 'runaway' in the language of the Creek Indians, that's all. Most of the Seminoles are Creeks. They come from two groups—the Mickasukee and the Muscogee—and they don't even speak the same dialect."

"If they're from two different tribes how do they get along?" The lieutenant wanted to know.

"Two different tribes!" The captain laughed.

"There are more than that. Some Cherokees, Choctaws, and others are with them. The few old Florida Indians left here, Calusas mostly, joined 'em also. Each band has its own chief, but they claim that they have just one king—Micanopy his name is. The different bands live separately, and each chief does what he pleases. They agree on only one thing—they all hate the Creeks up in Georgia. And because they couldn't get along with them, they left the tribe."

The lieutenant watched the young Indian, Osceola, as he walked away. He was slim and brown, not as dark as some Seminoles, and of average height. Now, moving with the ease of a panther, he disappeared into the forest of oak and palmetto beyond the fort.

Louis followed him with his eyes. Then he said slowly, "Some folks call that boy Powell, sir, for they say that his father is an English trader named Powell who lives in Alabama. I don't believe it."

"He doesn't look it—and that's a fact," replied the captain.

The lieutenant nodded. No one could watch the way the Seminole moved, or look into his face, and still think he was anything but a full-blooded Indian.

Around the army post people talked of Osceola. Some said that his grandfather was a Scottish trader named McQueen, who had married a Creek. Others believed that Osceola was the son of Powell and an Indian princess called Sally. Some said that Osceola's father was a warrior who was killed fighting Andrew Jackson's army. It was even said that Osceola, as a boy of nine or ten, had fought the white soldiers and Creek Indians in Georgia. At any rate, everybody knew that he could shoot a rifle with remarkable skill, despite the fact that he didn't own one.

Nobody seemed to know, even up in Washington, just how many Seminoles were in Florida. Old "Andy" Jackson hadn't had much trouble defeating a few of them in northern Florida in 1818, so he thought that the number was small. He found out differently later on, for in 1819 Spain sold Florida to the United States and it became a territory. Then General Andrew Jackson was made the first territorial governor and also the Indian agent.

Even for some years after that, Florida was unknown to most of the people in the United States, for it was strange and different. To begin with, it had a different shape. Then, too, it was thinly settled. If you could have stood on the Georgia border in the 1820's and looked down at the long peninsula, what would you have seen?

Well, to the west was Pensacola, a lively little Spanish kind of town. A little nearer was Tallahassee, just being started as the state capital. To the east there was a village called Cow Ford, later named Jacksonville for Old Hickory. Just south of Cow Ford, on the ocean, lay St. Augustine which was built on the spot where Ponce de Leon had landed. An ancient and a busy little city, St. Augustine was the center of Florida life.

Down below these north Florida settlements there spread a wilderness of lovely rivers and lakes

TALLAHASSEE
SUWANEE RIVER
JACKSONVILLE
ST. AUGUSTINE
FORT DRANE
FORT KING
COVE OF THE
WITHLACOOCHEE
FORT MELLON
BIG WAHOO
SWAMP
DADE'S MASSACRE
FORT BROOKE
TAMPA BAY
BATTLE OF
OKEECHOBEE
LAKE
OKEE
CHO
BEE
EVERGLADES
OSCEOLA'S
FLORIDA

overhung with myrtle and moss. If you could have seen far enough you would have noticed hammock land, where live oak, cedar, and sweet bay grew. You would have seen the scrub areas, with dense thickets of palmetto, and the gray swamps where dismal cypress trees stood in water. And still farther south, the far-flung Everglades spread miles of watery grasses.

All this country was guarded by a few army posts. One of the most important was Fort King in central Florida. At Tampa Bay, where De Soto had first set booted foot, a log blockhouse called Fort Brooke housed a few soldiers. They were needed to protect the people who were coming into the new territory.

Wealthy planters were moving into northern Florida with their slaves and setting out a few orange groves. Borderers, who were the poorer pioneers, were rattling down from Georgia in wagons filled with children and household goods. The men cracked long bull whips over their mules

Borderers from Georgia were rattling into Florida

or oxen, and were as ready to shoot an Indian as a panther.

Steps had to be taken to settle the problem of the Indians.

This was done at Moultrie Creek, when the Seminoles signed a treaty that gave them a big area of land in central and southern Florida. In return they agreed not to wander off to the coasts of the peninsula.

By 1828, when Andrew Jackson became President of the United States, trouble was slowly brewing in Florida. "Andy" Jackson was a hero to the people, but he didn't like Indians any better than the borderers did. Both the borderers and the planters wanted the Indians out of the way because they wanted the Indians' land.

The slave question gave these people another reason for their dislike of Indians. Slaves were constantly running away and joining the Seminoles. Although the Indians did not give the runaways their freedom, they treated them in a kindly way. Negro slaves could live in their own villages, and grow corn and tend cattle for Seminoles, who protected them.

But trouble was certainly coming! For one thing, slave catchers took the runaways north to sell whenever they could get them away from the Indians. For another thing, the brave men and women who were leading the hard lives of pioneers were determined to get their own land. How could they understand the Indian's hatred for those who wanted to take away his hunting grounds?

2

Peace Creek

Osceola moved from place to place as easily as a panther wanders through the forest. All his life the young Seminole had been a wanderer. His tribe, the Red Sticks, or Mickasukees, were fiercely independent, even more than most Seminole bands.

Osceola had been born in Alabama in 1804, not far from the place where the muddy water of the Chattahoochee River joined the clear brown stream of the Flint. When the Seminoles moved southward, Osceola and his mother Sally went with them to live on Peace Creek.

Osceola had no special standing in his tribe, for his father had not been a chief. His boyhood was the boyhood of all Seminole boys. When he was too big for his mother's back he toddled about the camp, learning to climb up on the platform floor of the chikee, or palm-thatched hut. There were about twenty of these huts in the village.

The huts were built around a cooking chikee that stood in the center. This was just a roof, without the two-foot-high floor. In the cooking chikee a fire always burned. It was made with big logs laid like spokes in a wheel, with the flames at the middle.

During rainy or cold weather, all the people sat on the logs. Women and children worked, and men rested from the hunt. Between the logs slept dogs, pigs, and chickens.

As the Seminoles grew and things happened to them, their names were often changed. Then, too, white men sometimes changed the names of Indians or translated them into English. To the white man Boleck was Bowlegs; Arpeika was Sam

The Seminole village was made up of palm-thatched huts

Jones; Coacoochee was Wildcat. Osceola was often called Powell. His name changed as he grew, but the one that remained his was really Assi-yohola—or Osceola.

"Assi" was the word for a drink that was black in color and bad in taste. At the Green Corn Dance, when the golden ears were ripe in June, each brave swallowed a gourdful of this ceremonial black drink. As the brave finished, he and the other warriors gave a loud cry:

"Yohola!"

Osceola's voice was musical and peculiarly

strong. So he was called Assi-yohola. To the white men this name sounded like "Osceola."

The Green Corn Dance was the sacred festival of the year. It was held after the village was swept, old cooking pots and old clothes were thrown away, and a new year had begun. The council of chiefs then tried those who had offended against the laws during the past year, and punished the guilty.

Men and women danced for days, and even the children sang their tribal songs. Seminoles could sing of the alligator in the mud bank, of the snake, the fox, of the great owl, and of hunting. Children sang the song of the rat as they played a game, and women crooned lullabies or sometimes a sad song of leaving.

All the people danced to the sound of drums and of rattles made of turtle shells. Then they feasted on meats, and on a mush of corn or of root flour called sofkee.

Osceola grew up believing that ghosts of departed warriors were near by, gray in the swaying moss of trees in twilight. He felt that he could hear demons in the hurricane winds, and the soft sighing of gentle spirits in warm breezes.

He and his brother Seminoles had a respect for snakes. They could smell a rattler, and avoid him. Because they let snakes alone, they were seldom poisoned.

Osceola hunted panther and bear, and could drop a squirrel with a single arrow. When he was old enough to make his own canoe he went with the men of his village into the swamp to cut down a cypress tree. The log was buried in the mud on Peace Creek with a special ceremony. Two years later, after it had been well seasoned in the mud, Osceola dug it up and brought it to the village.

When it was dry the other men worked on it with him. The ends were carefully shaped to form a long, low pointed canoe. Then the center of the log was burned out. Children tapped with sticks on the sides in order that the men might estimate the thickness of the wood as they

With his bow and arrow Osceola hunted animals in the forest

smoothed the inside. When the canoe was finished Osceola poled it on the shallow rivers and lakes.

It took patience to fashion a canoe of hard cypress wood. It took great physical endurance to play a ball game with baskets made of leather thongs fastened on the hand. Even women played with the deerskin ball, hitting it against two poles on the field. But the men's game went on for hours, with never a break in speed.

Seminoles had no wish to win against one another in anything, but they admired the man who had the most strength and skill. Among the tribesmen, Osceola became known as the strongest and best ball player.

Osceola was interested in the white man's ways. When Seminoles were forbidden to go to the coasts, he had to stay away from Fort Brooke on Tampa Bay, so he went to live near Fort King. He joined a band of Red Sticks in a village in the Wahoo Swamp, a hundred miles north of Tampa Bay. Here Osceola became a leader, for other warriors listened to him. He had two wives, as was the custom. He also had a horse, cattle, and corn fields. In his free time, he often went to Fort King to watch soldiers drilling.

Perhaps Osceola was preparing for the future, for he knew that his neighbors were unhappy and discontented. He heard the village men talking angrily about a settler who had robbed a Seminole of his cattle. They spoke of another white man who had whipped an Indian. They talked about slave hunters who raided the Seminoles' Negro villages. Osceola was friendly with white men at the fort—but he listened carefully, and forgot nothing.

3

He Speaks With Two Tongues

Osceola stepped softly out of the forest trail, and stood looking for a moment at Fort King. He saw the log fort inside a stockade fence, with the house of the Indian agent near by. The house and store belonging to the storekeeper, or sutler, was off some distance, near the edge of the woods.

Inside the fence, troops sat around in the heat of midday. There wasn't much for them to do. Off toward the river a limpkin bird gave its frightening cry. Osceola smiled a little as he saw a new recruit jump and look around him. It took a little while for these white men to get used to the roar of a bull alligator at night, or the scream of a panther in the swamp. Osceola had once gone back to his village to tell of a soldier who walked with his eyes on the ground all the time, watching for rattlers. That made the Indians laugh.

Now Osceola went toward the store and stepped quietly inside. As he was buying a piece of green cotton cloth for a new shirt, a soldier entered and said to the sutler, "Tell Osceola that General Thompson wants him."

The sutler called a Negro interpreter, who instructed Osceola to go to the office of the Indian agent, General Wiley Thompson. The General was an army officer who had been sent to Florida especially to deal with the Indians. He had no army command in the territory, for General Duncan Clinch was commander of the troops in Florida.

As Osceola entered the office, Thompson was saying to Lieutenant Graham, "I would give all the sand in Florida right now for a sight of the red clay hills of north Georgia!" He sighed as he stared through the windows at the shimmering heat waves on the parade ground. "Or St. Augustine! The cool salt breezes from the ocean—ah—and how I would like to sit on the verandah of my sister's home in the shade of a magnolia tree!"

"Your sister lives in St. Augustine, doesn't she?" the Lieutenant asked.

"Yes, her husband is a doctor there." Just then, General Thompson caught sight of Osceola in the doorway. "Tell him to come in, Graham."

Lieutenant Graham had lived with the Seminoles at different times and could speak their language. He especially liked and admired Osceola.

"Come in, Osceola," he urged. "The General has something to say to you."

"Yes," said Thompson, speaking carefully. "We have had a little trouble. I think that you may be able to help us, Osceola. Two young warriors from your band were seen stealing a cow from a settler on the edge of the reservation. Both men got away into the swamp. Now, as you know, the law gives me the right to have them whipped if they are caught. Ten strokes of the lash! I do not like to do this, for I know that now and then the settlers steal cattle from the Indians."

Osceola nodded gravely, his face very serious, and replied, "Many times they have taken our cattle and our horses. Many times our slaves are stolen. The complaints of the white men are carried to the right ears on wings of the wind, while those of the Indian are drowned in the storm."

The General agreed. "I know, and I try to stop it. The law of the United States forbids whites to steal Indian cattle. But more settlers are coming in. We cannot watch all of them."

"The laws of the Seminole also forbid stealing," said Osceola. "Seminoles obey tribal laws. But we lose many cows. And so some Indians take cows."

"This time, Osceola, the stealing was done by two braves from your village. Will you help us find them? In return for your help, I will promise not to whip them—that is, of course, if they return the cow."

Next day Osceola brought in the two young Indians and the cow

Osceola nodded slowly. "You are speaking the truth. This cow was not theirs. I will find them, and I know you will keep your word. Our council will punish the two men for stealing."

General Thompson was well satisfied, for he knew that the word of Osceola was dependable. This man was the most intelligent of the Indians who came to the fort, and he was listened to by his own people. There was no one else who would be able to find the Indians so quickly, or bring them in so easily.

Thompson also knew that the council would deal with the cattle thieves at the approaching Green Corn Dance. The Seminoles had a code of honor that differed from the white man's, but they lived up to it better than the whites did to theirs.

Next day Osceola brought in the two young Indians and the cow. As the Seminoles appeared, the settler from whom the cow had been stolen was lounging outside the fort, with several other borderers. There they sat with a jug of whiskey, waiting and spitting tobacco juice at a grasshopper.

When General Thompson saw the Indians, he stepped out of his office and thanked Osceola. But just as he turned the cow over to the men and told the Indians they could go, the white men jumped to their feet and began to swear and shake their fists. The man who owned the cow shouted:

"I'll teach you—your dirty, thieving redskins! Next time I catch you I'll horsewhip you myself!"

General Thompson stared thoughtfully at Osceola. This Indian was a friend to the whites, and his friendship was valuable to them. Perhaps a gift would help Osceola to understand that not all white men were like the shouting, threatening borderers. So when Osceola came in to the fort again General Thompson handed him a new rifle.

Osceola took it carefully, as a thing of great value, and looked intently at the General, saying nothing. Then he handed it back, thinking that he had been asked to admire the weapon.

"That is for you, Osceola," said the General. "You are a good friend. You have done favors for us many times. That is a present from me. Take it."

Osceola's head went up as his brown hands clasped the gun. His eyes flashed eagerly, and a warm smile lighted his face.

Later, as he walked out of the fort, he met Lieutenant Graham. The two walked along together. As they came to the trail leading to the swamp, Osceola turned to Graham and smiled again.

"I am the white man's friend, so long as he is my friend. You are my friend. But there are many who are not the Indian's friend." The smile left Osceola's face, and he was impassive again, although his eyes flashed.

"Last night one of my people lost a horse," the Indian went on. "I do not say to General Thompson, 'Bring in the white man who took the horse!' He would say that he could not. General Thompson speaks with two tongues."

"But he gave you this new rifle, Osceola," the

Lieutenant pointed out. "Surely you believe him to be friendly?"

"General Thompson is friendly now. But he does not punish the white man for stealing." Osceola smiled again and said good-bye to his companion.

As the Lieutenant walked back to the fort, he thought about the difficult situation in Florida. Graham knew that up in Washington, people in high places were saying that the Seminoles must be sent west and the land in Florida given to the whites. Would Thompson protect the Indians if there were real trouble? Perhaps Osceola was right. Perhaps Thompson did speak with two tongues. Anyway you looked at it, there was danger in the air.

4

The Westward Trail

"Send the Indians west! Send 'em all!"

That was what President Jackson said. That was the talk in Washington.

A large area of land in Oklahoma was the place chosen by the government to be Indian Territory for the tribes from the East. There they must go, to live together, tribe with tribe, regardless of their feelings toward one another. The Creeks and the Cherokees and all the others who were living east of the Mississippi would have to go across the big river. The Cherokees started the long walk westward, and thousands died on the way. They called it the Trail of Tears.

In the month of May, 1832, some of the chiefs of the Florida Indian bands met with Government representatives at Payne's Landing on the Oklawaha River. Here the chiefs made their marks on a treaty which provided that the Seminoles were to go west three years after the ratification of this treaty in Washington. A delegation of a few chiefs, with interpreters, would be sent to Oklahoma to look over the land.

The trouble that grew out of this treaty was caused by the fact that not every chief signed it. Those who had failed to sign did not feel bound by it. The delegation, they felt, was meant to be nothing more than a party that would report back on the desirability of the western territory as a place to live.

While out there, however, the Florida Indians in the little party signed an additional treaty without consulting their fellow tribesmen in Florida.

When these Indians returned home and realized that the Seminoles were angry with them, they said that they had not understood what they were signing. Furthermore, they did not like the West, and felt that they had been tricked.

Many of the most powerful Seminole chiefs denied ever signing anything, and soon the white man and the Indian began to look on each other as enemies. Down in central Florida, a Seminole who was caught outside of the reservation was to receive, according to Florida law, "not exceeding thirty-nine stripes on his bare back, and his gun taken away from him."

Every now and then a few Seminoles would raid a farm or burn a barn as revenge for ill treatment.

"Get those Seminoles west! They've got to go," declared "Andy" Jackson up in the White House.

In Florida the Indians said, "This is our land. We will not give it up. How can we live with the Creeks? We fought them and left them!"

Meanwhile, General Wiley Thompson, who as Indian agent was responsible for shipping the Seminoles to the West, was trying to get the different bands to go to Tampa Bay, where transports were lying in harbor.

Then, in 1834, the Payne's Landing treaty was ratified by the United States Senate. At once, Thompson sent out word for the chiefs to meet him at Fort King. Before they arrived, he had his desk brought out of doors, and a new treaty of removal laid upon it.

Thompson, standing behind his desk, watched the chiefs come in with their bands of young warriors. Old Micanopy, called the king, stood in the center in full dress. The Seminoles were no longer wearing the ancient buckskin dress of the Creeks. Instead, they had on brightly colored cotton shirts that came below the knees. Their leggings were decorated with colored strings, and around their necks and on their arms they wore silver ornaments. Turbans of red, green, and blue cotton were wound around their heads. In the turbans waved feathers of the egret from their native swamps, or ostrich plumes bought from traders. Thrust in their belts they carried scalping knives, tomahawks, small mirrors, combs, and little bags of paint.

The warriors stood waiting silently for their chiefs to speak. A well-built Negro, six feet tall, stepped forth as interpreter. This was Abraham, known as The Prophet. He had become so important in the tribe that Micanopy had given him his freedom and he had become a leader.

Around Micanopy stood chiefs Jumper, Cloud, Alligator, Charley Amathla, Black Dirt, and others. Not far away, Osceola watched and listened carefully as Abraham interpreted the words of General Thompson.

The General said solemnly, "The President of the United States, General Andrew Jackson, wants you to go to the West to live. You will have more cattle and horses. But first you must sign this paper. And then you must bring your cattle to me here, and we will pay you in gold. You must also give up your slaves. You must abide by the Treaty of Payne's Landing. The Great White Chief is strong. He says that you must go!"

The deep strong voice of Abraham put the words into gutteral Indian language.

The chiefs moved closer and muttered under their breaths. What were they to do?

Osceola's eyes darted quickly around the group. He felt the hesitation. Thompson sensed it too, and quickly came forward with a pen in his hand. He asked each chief to make his mark on the paper.

Osceola's hand went swiftly to his belt. He stepped toward the desk. His arm rose in the air, and the sun glinted on the steel of his knife blade.

"I care no more for General Jackson than for you," he shouted. "This is the only treaty I will ever make."

He plunged his knife into the paper, and then wrenched it free. Thompson stood still, frozen

"This is the only treaty I will ever make"

with surprise. Osceola walked back, and the air crackled with anger. Soldiers around the Indian agent grasped their rifles.

But the Seminole chiefs stood now with Osceola. They all turned in silence and went back into the forest.

5

A War Cry!

Once more Wiley Thompson called for a meeting of the chiefs for the purpose of signing an agreement. This time the Indians spoke violently against leaving Florida. In great anger, Thompson replied that henceforward the principal chiefs, including old Micanopy himself, would not be regarded as leaders by the United States.

On receiving word of this action, the Secretary of War wrote to Thompson saying that both he and President Jackson thought the declaration was a serious mistake and that it would cause trouble. However, they would leave matters in the agent's hand. Thompson at once ordered the army stores to refuse to sell gunpowder to the Indians.

General Thompson decided to do nothing about the treaty for a while. Perhaps he could talk to one or two of the chiefs privately, and win them over. After all, the General thought, Osceola was not a chief. Why should he have any lasting influence?

So as the spring advanced into summer Thompson had a talk with chiefs Charley Amathla and Black Dirt. Both of them listened without anger and seemed to be accepting the idea that the white man was too strong to be defeated by the Indians. Perhaps, after all, the western territory was a good place to live. Perhaps . . .

During this time, the other Indians did not often come to Fort King. When they did they bought more gunpowder than usual at the general store. This worried General Clinch, for he had bought up a lot of land and had started a plantation. He was also speculating in land, and did not want any trouble with the Indians.

Then distressing news came to Thompson. More barns had been burned by Indians at night. In August a dispatch rider, taking the trail from Fort King to Fort Brooke, was ambushed and killed—supposedly by Indians. Things looked bad. However, Thompson still hoped that the Indians would quiet down and finally decide to leave for the West.

His hopes came to an end one day when the sutler's store at Fort King was filled with men. Soldiers were buying tobacco and standing about talking, slapping mosquitoes, and speaking of the fever. Several farmers who lived on the edge of the Indian land were there, explaining that they had come in to look for stray cattle. A stranger, whose speech told that he came from South Carolina, was asking questions about the Seminole Negroes.

"Now where do they live?" he wanted to know. "Right with the Injuns, or in separate villages?"

One of the settlers pushed his hat back on his head and looked at the stranger warningly. "You'd better stay away from the Injuns. They won't stand for slave catchers. You'll find yourself dumped in a swamp to get eaten by the alligators, but you won't know about it because you'll be good and dead."

Suddenly the speaker's head jerked around at a soft sound in the doorway. Osceola came in, followed by one of his wives, Che-cho-ter, or Morning Dew. She was a slim brown girl who spoke English. Her father was a Seminole, but her mother was a Negro who had escaped to the Indians many years before.

Translating for her husband, Che-cho-ter said Osceola wanted to buy powder for his rifle.

"General Thompson says too much powder is being bought by Indians," the sutler replied. "No more will be sold."

"This here's a runaway slave girl," he said

Osceola spoke angrily. "We need gunpowder for hunting."

The stranger reached over and took Morning Dew by the arm.

"This here's a runaway slave girl," he said. "I've got her description in my book. I'll just take her along with me."

Osceola's hand grasped his knife, but before he

could raise it four men were on him, holding him.

A soldier ran to the fort, and soon General Thompson came striding into the store.

"What's the trouble here?" he snapped.

The storekeeper replied, "General, I followed your orders and wouldn't sell powder to this Indian. The slave trader here is taking his wife. Says he has her description as a runaway slave."

General Thompson frowned. This slave catching was a bad affair altogether—even if the people taken were really escaped slaves. If he allowed it at all, he made the Indians angry. If he didn't, the wealthy plantation owners complained about him to Washington. He was already in disfavor because the Seminole chiefs had not signed the treaty. This man, Osceola, was responsible for that and deserved no favors.

Turning a cold, set face to Osceola, Thompson said, "I can do nothing if the man claims that this girl is a runaway slave. I have no proof that she isn't."

Osceola burst into wild language. Four soldiers

grabbed his arms and held them behind him while the slave catcher led the girl away. As the wagon rattled off, General Thompson ordered Osceola put in prison in the stockade, with iron shackles on his ankles.

For two days Osceola sat silently. But his eyes burned. He did not eat, and if he slept nobody knew it.

When General Thompson came with an interpreter to the prison, Osceola stared at him as if he did not see him. Thompson whipped out, "Powell, I know you are the man holding up the signing of this treaty. If you will agree to persuade the chiefs to sign I will let you go free!"

Osceola turned his flashing eyes on the General and declared proudly, "My name is not Powell. I am not a slave. I am a full-blooded Mickasukee!"

The General, controlling his fury with some difficulty, turned on his heel and left. Still, there was one bit of news that made him believe the problem could be brought to a peaceful end—

Charley Amathla and Black Dirt had, at last, agreed to go west with their bands of Seminoles. So Thompson sent a Negro messenger to Charley Amathla's village on the Withlacoochee River to ask that the chief talk to Osceola.

Charley Amathla looked thoughtfully at the messenger, and then slowly said that he would come to the fort. When he walked into the prison room where Osceola sat, he received not a word or sign that the prisoner recognized him. Charley Amathla spoke solemnly.

"The white man is strong," he said sadly. "He can get what he wants. He wants our land here. There are too many white men. They are as thick as the leaves on the trees. We must go beyond the great river where the white man will leave us in peace."

Then Osceola spoke, and his words were like the hissing of a rattler. "We must go to the Creeks, our enemies, whom we left when we came here? Some day the white man will go there, too. Then where do we go? Into the sea?"

Charley Amathla replied, "If you will agree not to make trouble, to talk peace with the white man, General Thompson will let you go free. He gives his word."

"His word! The white man has a forked tongue," Osceola hissed.

After Charley Amathla left, Osceola sat silently, buried in thought. At the end of the sixth day he called the guard. Then he made signs that he wanted the interpreter, for he wished to talk peace.

The iron bands were struck from his ankles. He rose slowly and walked out of the prison. When General Thompson returned his knife and gun, Osceola took them silently and went slowly toward the forest trail that led to his village in the Wahoo Swamp.

With Lieutenant Graham, the General stood watching in front of the fort. They saw Osceola turn as he reached the trees. Then he threw back his head and in a mighty voice shouted a war cry:

"Yo-ho—ee-lo!"

General Thompson shivered. That cry was so

penetrating and so horrible! He could well believe the story that the war whoop of Osceola was unlike that of any other Indian. But why be concerned? Osceola was not a chief, and he did not appear to have any following of importance. The Indian agent shrugged and went inside. What he did not know was that Osceola had decided that Thompson's tongue was snakelike and cunning, and that cunning must be fought with cunning.

Not long after that Osceola came into the fort with seventy warriors. The interpreter declared that they had come to "make peace" and to agree to leave for the West. General Thompson replied that they were wise to agree to the plans of "Big Knife," the great warrior Andrew Jackson who was chief in Washington.

Osceola stood with his warriors around him, head proudly raised. His eyes flashed as the agent replied. Thompson thought that these warriors had been strangely silent. He watched them as they went off into the forest without a single friendly gesture. But at least they had complied with the promise Osceola had made. Sighing with relief, the General walked into his office to complete plans for putting the Indians on shipboard.

6

The Price of Freedom

In November, 1835, Charley Amathla received word from General Wiley Thompson that three ships were in the harbor of Tampa Bay, ready to receive the Seminoles who had agreed to go west. Charley told his little band that they were to go to Fort Brooke. They must prepare at once to leave their village on the Withlacoochee River. Then he gathered his cattle, and the small herds belonging to his people, and with the help of two young men, he drove the beasts to Fort King.

General Thompson came out to watch the cattle go into the government corral. He greeted

Charley Amathla with a hand clasp and a smile.

"I'm glad to see you here with the herds, Charley," said Thompson. "Are your people ready to leave for Tampa Bay?"

Charley nodded gravely, saying, "They will start tomorrow before light. We are putting out our fire and turning our faces to the West."

"Good. Black Dirt says that he and perhaps some other chiefs will join you there. Tell me, Charley, what of that wild Indian, Powell?"

Charley Amathla's face did not change its se-

Out of the bushes sprang Osceola and a band of braves

rious expression. He said nothing, so General Thompson continued:

"Does Powell have much influence? Are the chiefs with him?"

Charley looked straight at the General, speaking slowly. "Osceola has many young braves with him. More chiefs are listening to his voice now. They say they will never leave Florida."

Thompson handed Charley Amathla a small bag of gold coins in payment for the cattle, and walked slowly back into the fort. This man Powell, or Osceola, had an amazing will and personality. That war whoop! Never had he heard the like.

With their business finished, Charley Amathla and his two companions set off along the trail to their village on the river. Charley had placed the bag of golden coins in his belt, and they jingled a little as he walked. Overhead the sun was like a hot golden piece in the sky, although storm clouds were gathering in the southeast. It was storm season—but looking up, Charley thought the storm would not be bad enough to keep his band from their journey next day.

Underfoot the sand squeaked slightly as the quiet moccasined feet moved along the trail. A breeze suddenly sprang up, swaying the long strands of moss, rattling brittle palmetto leaves. Charley Amathla quickened his steps, anxious to get home before the rain broke. He felt uneasy too—and did not quite know why. Then, just as the little party reached a place in the trail where a thicket of scrub palmetto grew dense and green, dark clouds moved across the face of the golden sun.

A frightful war cry rose, quivered, and ceased. A volley of shots rang out. Charley Amathla and his companions fell dead on the trail. Out of the bushes sprang Osceola and a band of braves. They were in war dress, with their faces painted the red and black of destruction. Osceola watched as his band scalped the victims.

As he turned to go, Osceola saw one of his

men take the little bag of gold coins from the belt of the dead chief. Snatching the bag, Osceola emptied the coins into his hand. Then he flung them in all directions. The sun came out abruptly, and the coins glittered as they fell.

Osceola set his face toward the swampland along the river. His men followed as he stepped into the underbrush, and they did not look back to see where the gold had fallen.

7

Vengeance

After the death of Charley Amathla in November, an ominous quiet settled down around Fort King. Men moved away from the fort only in groups, and armed. Rations were so short that General Clinch took six companies twenty miles north to his own plantation. There the men harvested corn to add to their supplies.

The situation was growing more alarming every day, for settlers to the north were being killed or burned out. Clinch sent to Fort Brooke for reinforcements. Volunteers responded to General

Call at Tallahassee, and went out under his personal orders to protect the farms.

On December 28, 1835, General Wiley Thompson met Lieutenant Constantine Smith in front of the agent's office, and the two men walked slowly toward the house and store of Erastus Rogers, the sutler.

"I'm anxious about our situation here, Lieutenant," said Thompson. "Colonel Crane, left in charge with one company, could hardly defend the fort from an attack. It may come at any time."

"You think the Indians mean war?" Lieutenant Smith asked.

"I do indeed—they are too quiet. They haven't been into the fort since Amathla was killed. Trouble is," Thompson said, smiling wryly, "you can never tell what Indians are up to."

"Yes," the Lieutenant agreed. "And if they start anything, Clinch may attack from Fort Drane. But as for us, I wish those reinforcements would come from Fort Brooke."

Erastus Rogers, the sutler, welcomed them, and

they sat down to dinner with several other men who were his guests for the meal. The cook had a special dinner prepared, and the men remained for a while afterward, smoking cigars and talking. General Thompson was the first to rise and start back, accompanied by Lieutenant Smith.

As the two men stepped from the door and strolled toward the fort, the late afternoon sun was setting. The lonely cry of a water bird echoed, and was answered by another. Lieutenant Smith slapped a mosquito, remarking wryly, "You would think these pesky insects would die off now that winter is with us."

General Thompson laughed. "This is a paradise for mosquitoes. As for winter—how I would like to see the snow whitening the hills of north Georgia!"

A slight sound from the fringe of low palmettos brought the two men to a stop.

"What was that?" whispered the Lieutenant.

A single shot hit Wiley Thompson. He dropped to the sandy earth, a red stain spreading across his tunic. Lieutenant Smith knelt beside him, and then got up with a dazed expression.

"He's dead! He's——"

A series of shots sent birds whirring through the trees. Lieutenant Smith fell limply beside Thompson. Out of the forest sprang ten Indians in full war paint. Some of them fell on the two victims and took their scalps. Then when the leader beckoned, they crept up on the house of the sutler where the men still sat, feet stretched out under the table, talking lazily. As the Indians jumped through the door, two of the men leaped out of a window and ran for the fort. The other three were shot and scalped.

In the kitchen the old Negro cook took a horrified look into the dining room, and then she hid behind a barrel. Rogers had removed most of his goods to the fort for safekeeping. The Indians came into the kitchen, looked around in disgust at finding nothing, and then disappeared into the swamp.

The first volley of shots had brought the offi-

A single shot hit Wiley Thompson

cers within the fort to their feet, shouting commands. Nobody knew that General Thompson and the Lieutenant were outside. Men rushed to close the picket gates, reaching for their guns as they ran. Colonel Crane thought that the fort was being attacked by a great number of Indians. The sound of a shrill, penetrating war cry sent a shiver down his back. The cry was followed by shots from the sutler's house, and then the many long-drawn whoops of victory from the Seminoles.

Crane and a captain, with a dozen armed soldiers, ran out to give help to their friends in the sutler's house. In the path they came on the bodies of General Thompson and Lieutenant Smith.

"Osceola?" asked the colonel grimly.

"Osceola," the captain agreed through set teeth. "And it looks as if he shot the General with the very rifle that he gave him."

The war was on!

8

Disaster

On the same day that General Thompson was killed by Osceola and his band, a detachment of a hundred troops was on the way northward from Fort Brooke to Fort King. This was the reinforcement for which the anxious men had been waiting. The troops marched in a column of route, or double file. They were followed by four horses pulling a six-pounder cannon and a team of oxen drawing a supply wagon. A rear guard and an advance guard completed the formation.

They had been on the march for three days, fording rivers, passing around lakes, following the sandy wagon road over the slight rises of the Florida countryside. During the first two days the troops traveled over a road that wound through dense palmetto hammocks where brush grew head high. Here the men kept careful watch, especially after they found that a log bridge over the Hillsborough River had been burned. No sign of Indians was seen after that. The men began to feel easier, for now on the fourth day's march the road, which was barely more than a trail, wound through more open country.

Major Dade, the commander of the reinforcements, rode forward to join the advance guard a quarter of a mile ahead of the main body of troops. He looked with sympathy at the marching men, who wore their coats buttoned over their cartridge belts because of the sudden chilly weather.

"You'll get a three-day rest at Fort King, boys," he called out, "and a good supply of rations!"

The men smiled. Although it was only eight o'clock in the morning, they were ready for a

Again the Indians attacked Major Dade's reinforcement troops

rest. Some of them who had just landed from ships lying in Tampa Bay were not used to such long marches.

Suddenly, from a clump of bushes, a volley of shots plowed into the advance column and the left flank of the formation. At the same moment a war whoop rose horribly and quivered in the air. Shots rang out again. Indians were hidden behind every bush and tree. Major Dade's horse wheeled violently and fell with its rider. Both were killed instantly.

During the attack, more than half of the troops fell. A private named Clark looked about wildly, for all the men who had been near him had been killed or wounded. The troops who survived dashed for the nearest trees, and fired from behind them. Until now Clark had not seen an Indian. As the soldiers fired, however, he could see here and there the heads of Seminoles, with feathers nodding in the turbans above their war paint.

Lieutenant Basinger had the cannon wheeled up and fired round after round of canister shot.

causing the Indians to withdraw. Captain Gardiner gave orders to have trees cut and a breastworks erected. Some of the soldiers ran to their fallen companions and got their ammunition and weapons. Just as the logs were put into a triangular protection, placed about knee high, the Indians attacked again from the grass and bushes.

Men and horses were dying on the road and in the low grass. The few men who were still able to shoot lay huddled behind the little log protection. From there, they continued to direct a sharp attack at the Indians.

The Seminoles, led by their king, Micanopy, by Chief Alligator, and by a young and active chief called Jumper, were creeping forward to surround the embattled soldiers. The cannon boomed again, but as the men were loading for the fiftieth discharge, their lighted match went out. So the last charge was never fired.

The few men left behind the logs stretched out and continued to fight until mid-afternoon. Just as the Indians closed in, the ammunition gave out.

Clark, who by some miracle was one of the last men shot, dropped over the bodies and pretended to be dead. As he lay wounded, he heard the Indians talking. They took the weapons of the defeated troops, but did nothing else to the dead or wounded.

Clark lay there as if dead until nightfall, when he crept away and started for Tampa Bay. For three days, with a severe wound in his shoulder, he staggered through wet swamp and dry hammock land, sometimes pursued by howling wolves.

How he reached the fort nobody could ever understand, but on December 31st he crawled into sight of the log stockade. Two other privates, both wounded, reached Fort Brooke also, but died later. Clark was the only real survivor of the battle known as Dade's Massacre, except for an officer's dog which came into the fort with a wounded shoulder.

Across the river from Fort Brooke several small bands of Seminoles were encamped. They had agreed to be shipped to the West, and had appeared, hungry and cold, not long before Dade's ill-fated march northward. Troops were sent out to guard them from attack, for it was feared that Black Dirt and the other chiefs who had signed the agreement were in danger of losing their lives. But nothing further happened near Tampa.

The officers and men at Fort King did not receive the news of Dade's defeat for several weeks, for all communication with the fort had been cut off. When Chief Alligator was captured more than a year later he told the officers at Fort Brooke that the attacks had been carefully planned.

He said that the detachment under Dade had been watched by the Indians all of the way. The troops had been attacked when they approached the big swamp, for the Indians knew that escape into the swamp would be easy for them if they should be defeated. According to Alligator, 180 warriors took part in the attack, and of these three were killed and five wounded.

In Washington President Jackson was furious when the news reached him, but nobody, including Old Hickory, thought that there were enough Seminole braves to fight for long. In Florida the troops in scattered little forts grimly prepared for attack.

9

Cove of the Withlacoochee

The clear dark water of the Withlacoochee winds through swamp and forest toward the Gulf of Mexico. About twenty miles from Fort Drane, the river makes a broad bend like an arm curved around a piece of wooded land. This was known as the Cove of the Withlacoochee. Here the white man had never come. Here the hostile Seminoles made headquarters. Scouts reported this to General Clinch. But since the warriors came and went all the time, the exact number in the cove could not be known.

About Christmas time, as Osceola was preparing to kill General Thompson, and while Chief Jumper and Alligator were talking old King Micanopy into ambushing Major Dade's troops, General Clinch was at Fort Drane. With him were Lieutenant Graham and six companies of regulars from Fort King. Also at Fort Drane were General Call and his Florida volunteers, who had been sent out by the governor to protect settlers. Neither Clinch nor Call had yet heard about the deaths of Thompson, Dade, and the men under them.

The two generals had a conference. Clinch had to make a decision.

"The Mickasukees are on the warpath," said Clinch to General Call. "You say they are attacking settlers in the north, and that you found burned-out houses?"

"Yes," Call replied, "and some men and women have been killed and scalped. However, I think that in all cases very small war parties did the damage."

"Yes—the Mickasukees are influencing the

others. If we can surprise the hostiles in the Cove of the Withlacoochee, I believe we can stop a real war from starting. Can you march with us?"

"Well——" Call shook his head doubtfully. "My volunteers signed up for only a few weeks. They want to go home. Most of them have only a few days more in their terms of service."

General Clinch shook his head, and frowned. "In that case we must attack at once. If we can inflict a decisive defeat on the hostiles now, the Seminoles will go in greater number to Tampa Bay. They are afraid of Jumper, Alligator, and Osceola."

The decision was made, and the troops—both regulars and volunteers—were on the march before daylight next day. General Call was in command of men who knew very little about military tactics. But they had lived in the wilderness all their lives, and knew the ways of the Indian. These volunteers traveled fast and light, with no excess baggage. For this reason, General Call grew irritated at General Clinch's regular army men who moved slowly because they were hampered by baggage trains and packs.

It took them two days to reach the place where the scout had reported an easy ford across the stream. They were disappointed to find that there was no ford. Instead, the river was fast and deep. If they were to surprise the Seminoles in their camps, a crossing must be made rapidly. Nothing seemed possible except an old Indian dugout canoe resting on the far bank. Two men swam across to get it.

The troops had arrived at dawn of the third day, but by noon men were still crossing the river in that one canoe, seven at a time. General Clinch took his regulars over first. His 200 men were crossing when a withering fire broke on them from the scrub and swamp. As the men landed, they ran for cover and formed their lines, returning the fire.

Volunteers began crossing the river in the canoe, but at the slow rate that was necessary the 400 men could not get across the swift river in time to be of help. They couldn't swim over without wetting their weapons. Although they continued to cross in the canoe, seven at a time, most of them had to remain on the opposite bank, helplessly watching the battle. General Call, who had gone over, shouted to his men to cut logs and build a bridge. Then he took his few volunteers into the hot fire of the Indian attack.

Seminoles crept closer, from tree to tree. Lieutenant Graham heard a chilling war cry, and knew that Osceola was the war-leader of the Indians. He had taken his stand behind a tree, but Graham saw him step forth every now and then to fire, and each time he brought a soldier down. Osceola wore a scarlet belt over his green war dress, and the black and white plumes curved proudly from his headdress.

Suddenly Graham knew that Osceola's sharp eyes had found and recognized him. The Indian, deliberately aiming his rifle at another man, ordered his warriors not to harm Graham. Never-

Osceola stepped forth every now and then to fire

theless, Graham was hit in the arm by a stray bullet and had to leave the battle from loss of blood.

Osceola was not dislodged from his stand until several volleys from a whole platoon had cut the tree to pieces. Then he moved back into the swamp with his warriors. The Seminole force was made up of about 250 men, commanded by Osceola and Alligator.

During the afternoon Clinch ordered retreat. This seemed impossible at first, but Call's men worked feverishly at throwing a rough bridge across the stream. When the Indians withdrew into the swamp to reload, the soldiers crossed the logs as fast as they could. As the last detachment went over, the war whoop rose again, and the Indians crept forward to attack the men on the bridge.

When the surviving troops, carrying their wounded, returned to Fort Drane, the volunteers left for their homes. The regular army men now knew that the number of Seminole warriors was much greater than they had expected. This wasn't going to be easy.

10

"I Am a Warrior!"

War rushed across Florida like a roaring forest fire. It never flamed up long in any one spot, but broke forth and died down first in one place, then in another. Bands of hostile Indians roamed at will, and United States soldiers marched from their stockaded forts to search them out.

In northern Florida, a man would come running at the scream of his wife, to find his barn on fire. Settlers riding mules, driving wagons, or trudging on foot would appear at scattered forts and beg for protection.

At the mouth of the Hillsborough River on

Tampa Bay, friendly Seminoles who had resigned themselves to leaving camped and waited patiently for ships to come for them. As the year 1836 progressed through the cool winter months, the few plantation owners south of St. Augustine fled to the ancient town. With them were their families and slaves. Some slaves were running away to join Indian bands, and were reporting the movements of the troops to Osceola.

The Seminoles, with their methods of getting information and planning attacks, had become a well-organized group. Chief Jumper was the "sense-keeper" or adviser for the head chief, Micanopy. Osceola was the acknowledged "head war leader," known throughout the wilderness country for his boldness, energy, and skill. When Osceola was leading a war party, no quarter was given to the enemy, but no women and children were ever harmed.

"I make war against white warriors," he said proudly, "for I am a warrior. I do not fight squaws and papooses."

Osceola never forgot a real friend and never forgave an enemy. He was furious with anger when he heard that Lieutenant Graham had been wounded, even though by chance. Osceola himself was also wounded in the hand in that battle, although he continued to fight until the troops retreated. The military skill that he had learned by watching the troops at Fort Brooke and at Fort King was very useful to him.

Then a battle took place that spread a fantastic rumor about the Seminole warrior, causing some people to say that he was a West Point graduate. It had been some months since the troops had met hostile Indians in actual combat, for the war soon became one of quick attacks from ambush and rapid disappearances into the forest or swamp. For the Indians it was skirmish and retreat. For the troops it was a march accompanied by baggage wagons and laden with packs—and then a failure to find the Indian marauders.

One morning Colonel Pierce's company moved

War broke forth in one place after another

forward just as the sun rose above the trees. His scouts had reported that Indians had stripped a corn field, and the colonel wanted to catch them. As the soldiers approached a stand of sugar cane, they saw dark shapes among the tall stalks. Instantly a warning gun was fired by an Indian lookout. The advancing troops shivered at the sound of Osceola's shrill war cry.

As the soldiers fell into attack formation, the Indians jumped forward at Osceola's command. They dropped their bundles of sugar cane as they ran, and reached for their rifles. Along the edge of the field where the grass was low, they formed a line of defense, for they were considerably outnumbered. The air was heavy with warnings of rain, and smoke from a burning brush fire made drifting misty clouds which swept down over the field.

Colonel Pierce and his men advanced, firing as they came. Their fire was returned by the Indians. The Colonel could hardly believe that he had, at last, closed with Osceola and some of his braves in an open battle. But Osceola understood the tactics of the white fighter, and he planned a maneuver of his own. If the fog continued to come to the aid of the Indians, the plan must succeed.

Keeping the front line of the enemy engaged in a sharp fire, Osceola ordered two flanking movements to separate the troops and cut off their retreat. Just as the Indians crept forward on the right and left flanks, a quick breeze sprang up. The fog rose rapidly, and the maneuver was discovered.

Osceola gave a high cry for retreat. His warriors slipped into the cane and moved back toward a hammock of high land overgrown with trees and bushes.

Colonel Pierce rallied his surprised men, and pursued the Indians. But when the troops reached the hammock, the Seminoles had disappeared as quickly and as silently as the white, smoky fog that had betrayed them.

Colonel Pierce shook his head in astonishment as he sat that night in the fort, talking to a captain.

"I can't understand it," said the colonel. "Anyone would think that the Indian warrior Osceola—or Powell, as they sometimes call him—had graduated from West Point. Where did he learn tactics? No Indian I ever heard of could fight like that. Had it not been for that little swift breeze, we would have been done for. As it was we lost more men than the Indians."

The captain gave a wry grimace. "All I know, Colonel, is that Osceola is very clever. He can't speak English, but he seems to know ahead of time what the white soldier will do. Some say this war will soon be over—but I say no Indian chief in this country has ever fought like Osceola. The war with him will not be easy, or quick to end." He sighed, for like all of the troops in Florida, he was homesick.

The swamp was the Seminole's friend. Indians could hide safely among the gray dead-looking cypress trees, with their knobby "knees," standing in dank water. Soldiers didn't like invading the swamps, where snakes lived on the islands and alligators thrust their snouts up out of the mud. But Seminoles knew how to live with the swamp creatures.

From time to time the soldiers found a Seminole village. It would always be deserted, for the women and children seemed to know when to disappear. And then the troops would burn the palmetto-thatched chikees—they made fine blazes, too—and take away the cattle and horses.

Seminoles had formerly lived as settled Indians in Florida, with towns and with herds of cattle

Indians could hide safely among the cypress trees of the swamp

and horses. Now they were wanderers, hiding deep in swamps on islands.

When troops did venture into the mysterious shade of the "slews," as borderers called the swamps, Seminole women and children hid in water to their mouths. They put leaves over their heads, and the little babies never uttered a cry to betray them.

If a child should give away a hiding place, the mother might even kill it to protect the band. But Seminole children learned to grow up silently, with hatred for the whites, and with the determination never to give in.

White soldiers didn't find the war in Florida easy or pleasant. Malaria rose from the swamps, throwing them into shaking chills and fevers. People were not to learn for a generation that malaria and the dreaded yellow fever were caused by mosquitoes.

They knew now, however, that they had a skillful and a brave foe in Osceola. They knew that if it were not for Osceola, the other chiefs would probably agree to go west. But they also knew that Osceola would never leave—that his anger and his will to resist burned like a fire within him, and spread to the other warriors.

11

Peace or War?

General Edmund Gaines, commander of the southeastern military area, with headquarters in Memphis, Tennessee, had no sooner received word that the Seminole war had broken out than he sent out a call for volunteers. From New Orleans he sailed with eight companies of 1,100 men in all. Traveling in three steamboats, they arrived in Tampa Bay in early February, 1836, and marched into the Florida wilderness at once.

Since the disastrous battle between the Indians and Dade's troops, the two forts had been short-handed, cut off from each other, and in fear of an attack by the Indians.

Although Dade's men had met their deaths nearly two months before, they had not yet been buried, and so General Gaines came upon them lying exactly as they had fallen. A remarkable fact was that every man was accounted for, and not one of them had been robbed. Even their watches and money remained. Nothing had been taken except their weapons and the coat of their commander, Major Dade.

After the bodies were buried in two graves and the cannon placed over them, General Gaines went on with his troops to Fort King. He had rations for only ten days and needed to secure food at the fort.

But Fort King was not only short of troops, it was also short of food. General Gaines decided to march back to Tampa Bay along the shore of the Withlacoochee River. There he hoped to defeat the Seminoles in force, and thus end the war quickly.

Meantime trouble was brewing among the commanding officers. General Clinch had been in command in Florida, but the War Department, on hearing the report of the Dade disaster, had sent General Winfield Scott down to take Clinch's place. General Gaines, in command of the whole southeastern area, had moved from New Orleans to Florida, although he had received no instructions to do so.

There was thus a good deal of confusion, and some anger at this mixed-up situation. Only the Seminoles profited by it. As far as they were concerned, the more confusion in the United States command, the better.

The shortage of food was another source of trouble. Gaines sent to Fort Drane for supplies, and received enough food to last his men a few days. The troops arrived at the spot on the river where Clinch had made his unfortunate crossing. Here they heard a volley of shots from the opposite side, and the fearful sound of the war whoop. General Gaines sent a messenger back to Fort Drane asking General Clinch to bring a force down on the other side of the river, and take the Indians by surprise. This might end the war, Gaines thought.

His men were attacked again as they marched down the Withlacoochee. As a party was cutting timber and making canoes for crossing the river, the Indians closed in, firing from every side except the river.

General Gaines prepared to dig in and defend himself.

"Sounds like a bigger attack than I expected," he said to his officers. "Indians must have come in great numbers since yesterday."

"Yes, sir, they have followed us all along the river, and have evidently sent word to gather in force."

The battle continued for two hours. One soldier was killed, and thirty-three men were wounded. The General was hit in the mouth, suffering the loss of a tooth. A captain ran to him shouting, "General, are you badly hurt?"

Gaines's men were attacked while cutting timber

Gaines, hardly able to speak, but with a half smile in his eyes, said hoarsely, "No–it's not much. Just my lip–and a tooth! It was very unkind of those rascals to take away a tooth that I value so highly."

That night the Indians seemed to disappear, for there was no sound or sight of them. Nor was there any sign of them during the next two days.

Gaines thought it best to remain there until Clinch could send relief.

The men waited, and their supplies grew so low that they were compelled to kill all of their horses for food. Several days passed. Then, when the woods were unnaturally quiet, and not a movement betrayed the presence of an Indian foe, the high, shrill war cry of Osceola was heard. The soldiers grasped rifles and watched intently. Fire poured upon them from all sides as the Seminoles crept slowly closer.

After that, every day, an attack would come at an unexpected time. Firing would start, and then suddenly cease. When the troops had been besieged for nearly a week, a high call was heard one evening just as darkness fell upon the woods and the river.

"Who goes there?" shouted an officer.

"We want to talk!" came the answer. "We want to stop fighting!"

General Gaines listened intently. Was this a trick? He knew that the Seminoles would use trickery when they wanted to get out of a bad situation. But he knew, too, that they could be depended upon to act honorably under a flag of truce. That they held sacred in their own code.

Making up his mind quickly, the General gave an order to the officer of the guard, who called:

"If you want to stop fighting and talk peace, send a messenger tomorrow morning, in daylight, with your interpreter. Bring a white flag of truce! You may come and go in safety."

The Seminoles' answer came after a few moments. "Very well. We want to have a friendly talk and shake hands."

All night the troops remained awake, listening to the hoot owls in the trees, the bullfrogs in the river, and the queer sounds of tropical birds. As the sun rose, a group of about 300 Seminoles advanced from the forest, and stood waiting silently. One of them held a stick with a white cloth tied to it.

The weary soldiers tightened their nerves, on

guard against a surprise assault. They knew that the bushes and trees around them concealed Indians. Both the soldiers and the Indians waited for a moment, tense with suspicion.

Slowly Osceola advanced with two other chiefs. The interpreter called out that they wished a talk, for they did not want to fight any more. Gaines sent a staff officer out to meet them.

"Our chief, Micanopy, wishes to make peace," said Osceola. "We have agreed in council that we will not fight you here any longer if you will leave the Withlacoochee River."

By order of General Gaines, the officer told him, "A large force of United States troops is on the way. With them, we can defeat the Seminoles. If we agree to your terms, will you go with all your people south of this river? Then, later, will you come to a parley with the agents of the United States government? If so, we will withdraw, and you will not be harmed."

The chiefs went back to consult with Micanopy

and the council. Then once again they came forth to meet the officer on the grassy open spot near the river.

"Our king, Micanopy, and our council of chiefs agree to do these things. We——"

Shots rang out! The warriors near the trees fled into the forest. From the north appeared a column of several hundred men in army blue. They advanced at a run, shooting at the Indians as they came. Osceola and the other peace delegates ran like deer for cover. The camp was thrown into wild confusion, with men shouting and yelling. General Gaines greeted the column angrily, and yet with relief. General Clinch spurred his horse forward and barked out that he had brought food and reinforcements for the half-starved men.

The hungry troops threw themselves on the ground and ate ravenously. Their bearded, dirty faces showed the strain of the siege. They rested there two days, while the generals conferred in their tent. Around the camp the woods were quiet, except for the sound of the river and of the birds.

The men knew that the Indians believed the mistaken attack to have been a planned trick. So the weary scouts searched for Indians, and listened for every slight warning of their approach. No Indians appeared, and the troops marched back to Fort Drane without incident. General Gaines then turned over his men to General Clinch, and returned to his command post on the Mississippi River.

12

Tricks?

The Florida war was baffling to the United States soldiers and to their commanding officers. Troops were sent down to Florida in small numbers, and then withdrawn. Nobody seemed to know what was happening—except that no white man's life or property was safe. No wonder the white borderers were in a panic!

In that first year of the war, alarms sprang up from east and west in Florida. People trembled, and gathered at forts to discuss the news.

"Did you know that the collector of the port at Charlotte Harbor was killed by the Seminoles?"

"I heard that Injuns burned Fort Drane!"

"Sure did. They set fires to Auld Lang Syne, too—General Clinch's plantation. And burned seventy hogsheads of sugar!"

"There was a fight at Micanopy Town! The lighthouse at Cape Florida was burned, and the keeper just barely got away with his life! Fort Drane has been abandoned. The army isn't going to rebuild it. Not far from there a baggage train, traveling with an escort of twenty-six dragoons, was destroyed."

People fled to St. Augustine and to the forts. If they remained in their homes they kept a shotgun within reach, and somebody stood watch by day and by night. Men were afraid to work in their fields, and women shivered on their corn shuck mattresses at night.

"Osceola!"

The very word turned settlers pale with fright.

After the battle with General Gaines, the Indians had fought another against General Winfield Scott, sent down by order of the Secretary of War.

The situation in regard to commanding officers was not clear to anybody. After Scott, General Jesup took command.

A campaign against the Seminoles in the autumn of 1836 was a failure. Invasions into the Wahoo Swamp had produced little more than a chance to burn a few scattered Indian towns. No real battles were fought.

Every now and then a truce would take place. Indians would come to an army camp and act in a friendly manner. This would lead the army offi-

Every now and then a truce would take place

cers to believe that the Seminoles were now going to agree to leave Florida. But the Indians always came feeling that a friendly talk would lead to a compromise. They might even get terms that would give them a small part of Florida!

In May, 1837, several of the more important bands of hostile Seminoles came to General Jesup at Fort Brooke. Micanopy, Jumper, Alligator, Abraham, and Wildcat pitched their camps along the river. The General thought that these leaders would take their people west when the vessels arrived for them. On the other hand, the Indians believed that the army would let them take along their Negro allies and slaves.

Then two things happened. First the officers in charge, ignoring the promise to let the Negroes alone, allowed slave hunters to search the Indian camps along the river. At the same time measles broke out and spread rapidly.

One morning in June, the army found that the camps were empty. Every Seminole had disappeared into the woods. Officers believed that

Osceola had come secretly and persuaded the Indians to leave. When twenty-four transports arrived in the harbor, there were no passengers for them, but General Jesup ordered the vessels to wait, hoping that the matter could be settled.

Because it was now summer, Jesup was handicapped by lack of troops; the volunteers had gone home after a short term of service. Jesup knew that the Indians had an even more serious problem —they had little food, for they couldn't stay in their villages long enough to grow much. They were also having trouble getting skins to barter to smugglers on the coast for gunpowder. Traders couldn't get to them easily with cotton cloth. They were growing ragged. Perhaps they were tired of holding out—but then again maybe they were not giving up so easily.

At Fort Mellon on Lake Monroe, Jesup spoke to Lieutenant-Colonel Harney, commander of the fort. When Harney reported that the Indians wanted another "talk," the General ran his hand through his hair angrily.

"How can anybody understand them!" he exclaimed in exasperation. "First you see 'em, then you don't! Burn their crops, and they eat coontie roots and trapped game. They get thin and ragged, but they can live on the country."

The Lieutenant-Colonel grinned and sighed. "Just as we feel like giving this whole good-for-nothing country to them, old Micanopy strolls into camp and says he wants to 'talk'."

Jesup pushed back his chair and got up wearily. "It's probably a trick. They will eat and sleep here, and then go. But we can't afford not to listen. Maybe this time they mean it. Get the camp ready for them, Colonel."

Lieutenant-Colonel Harney put Captain Vinton in charge of the Indian camp at the fort.

Soon small bands of Seminole men, women, and children arrived. Their solemn chiefs sat and watched a ball game every day. Women stood at the little dock, staring at a steamship that made regular trips down the St. John's River and into the lake. Although the Indians were enjoying themselves, Jesup was anxious to get them on their way west quickly. Fevers were raging in the fort, and he gave orders to abandon it for the summer.

Captain Vinton was amazed one day to see even Osceola come into camp and walk about, observing everything with his strange quick glances.

Lieutenant-Colonel Harney remarked to General Jesup, "This looks like a real armistice, General. We have Jumper and Wildcat here, as well as Micanopy and Osceola."

But day after day passed, "talks" were held with the army officers, and nothing was decided. The chiefs had councils among themselves—councils in which Osceola's voice was often heard. After a ten-day visit, which the Indians seemed to enjoy, soldiers woke to a quiet camp. The Seminoles had vanished again—back into swamps and dense palmetto scrubs.

Jesup pounded his desk with his fist. "This means war again! That man Powell is responsible. I am sure that Micanopy would have taken his people west. Maybe Powell and Wildcat forced him to leave."

Vinton looked thoughtfully at Jesup, and Harney sighed wearily. Then he said, "Osceola wouldn't have to kidnap Micanopy, General. Osceola has a power of persuasion that can draw the young braves with him any time. The old chief is weak. He can't stand up against the young warriors. Osceola is a remarkable man."

"Remarkable or not, we will get him," muttered the General grimly. "If they can play tricks, so can we."

Fort Mellon was abandoned for the time being. The army forces left, some on foot, some by steamer up the beautiful St. John's River. And then Indians came back to walk sure-footed and unafraid through the deserted fort.

13

A Flag of Truce

Micanopy, the head chief of the nation of Seminoles, was not a strong leader. King Philip, his brother-in-law who was sixty years of age, was a chief with a stronger will. Very much like him in this respect was his son, Wildcat. Osceola had a liking and a respect for old King Philip.

In September four slaves, who had been captured by the Indians some months before, escaped from Philip's band and reached St. Augustine. They offered to guide the troops to Philip's camp.

General Hernandez, commanding the St. Augustine area, gave marching orders to two companies of dragoons, or mounted infantry; one company of artillery; and two companies of Florida militia. They set out with him through deep sands, swamps, and pine barrens. Thirty miles to the south Hernandez's troops came to Bulow's plantation. There they camped until nightfall near the ruins of a mill and a mansion that had been burned sometime before by the Seminoles.

Ten miles farther on, a part of the troops moved quietly up on the destroyed plantation buildings of Dunlawton, where they saw Indians around a campfire. Lieutenants Whitehurst and Pelitier concealed their volunteers on either side, while the regulars charged into the camp on horses. The whole Indian party was surrounded and captured without a casualty on either side. One young boy, a son of Philip, escaped into the dark bushes. Philip and his little band were taken to St. Augustine and locked in the prison cells at old Fort Marion.

That same night, a hundred of the soldiers waded into a swamp, fought a short but sharp battle with a band led by Uchee Billy, and took the Indians prisoners. It seemed to the military men that at last the Seminoles might be losing their powers of resistance. In the prison fort there were fifty-three Indians, including five chiefs.

On hearing that his father had been captured, Wildcat went boldly to St. Augustine under a flag of truce and asked to speak to King Philip. General Hernandez gave permission, for he saw that the old chief was very weary of fighting. He thought, too, that Philip might encourage Wildcat to give up. The General was surprised and pleased when Wildcat promised that he would talk with other chiefs and would bring them in for a parley with Hernandez.

Two weeks later, about the middle of October, Wildcat came back to the city with news that other chiefs were encamped near by. He brought a peace pipe and the white feather of the wild egret to the General. These were gifts from Osceola, which meant that he would meet Hernandez for a talk.

General Hernandez looked at the peace pipe

and feather, knowing them to be a request for safe-conduct for negotiations. He turned to Wildcat and said:

"Tell Osceola that I will talk with him. Tell him to meet me a mile south of Fort Peyton, at the old Indian camp."

General Hernandez sent word of the proposed meeting to General Jesup, who returned secret orders to him immediately. Hernandez prepared to leave.

Osceola nodded gravely as Wildcat gave him the message from Hernandez. But he did not smile. There was seldom a smile on his face these days, for conditions among the Seminoles were very bad. They were ragged, and many were almost without clothing. They had little to eat except a mush made from the coontie root and small game that could be trapped. Their Negro allies were almost starving, and some were running away to white settlements.

The Seminoles had been hunted down from swamp to hammock land and through the pine barrens not only by troops, but also by other Indians—Choctaw, Creek, and Chickasaw—hired to pursue them. A bounty of $500 was paid to anyone bringing in a Seminole warrior.

As Osceola put on his ceremonial dress for his meeting with the General, he turned sadly to an old friend and said:

"I may not see you again."

When his friend asked the reason for this statement, Osceola said nothing. He was beginning to feel that perhaps he and his whole people had no future but destruction. Yet he did not intend to submit, for he still had hopes that his meeting near Fort Peyton with General Hernandez would bring about a compromise.

Fort Peyton was eight miles south of St. Augustine, and the meeting place was a mile from the fort. Osceola approached with seventy warriors, followed by their wives and children. Beside Osceola walked a warrior carrying a white flag on a stick. Awaiting the delegation was General Hernandez, standing stiffly erect, with 200 troops behind him.

As the Indian war chief stepped forward, his head was raised proudly. The black-and-white plumes seemed scarcely to move with his even, lithe stride. His flashing eyes shifted about from the face of one soldier to another. His lips tightened, for he could feel danger.

The General began to question Osceola.

"Why have you come to talk? What do you want to do, Osceola? We will not accept anything but a surrender. Why haven't you brought the captive slaves to turn over to us?"

Osceola stood as straight as the pine trees behind him. He stared at the General as the interpreter spoke. He said nothing. General Hernandez frowned. He thought of the definite instructions he had received from his commanding officer, General Jesup. But he asked again:

"Have the chiefs held a council and decided to go to the land provided for the Seminoles in the

Everybody wanted to see the captured war leader

West? Why haven't the chiefs come to tell me, and to surrender?"

Osceola listened to the words of the General. He murmured something in a low tone.

Hernandez demanded of the interpreter, "What did he say?"

"He says that his throat feels choked," the interpreter replied. "He cannot answer these questions. He——"

General Hernandez raised his arm abruptly in a prearranged signal. The troops closed in swiftly on the Indians, grasping them roughly by the arms and taking their rifles. Osceola was seized so violently that he almost fell.

General Jesup arrived as the Indians were being marched between a double file of soldiers to St. Augustine. It was by the order of the commanding general that Osceola had been taken under a flag of truce. Osceola walked quietly between the files of soldiers, his face stony with grief. Yet his eyes burned with anger and hatred.

An excited dragoon came galloping through the town to tell the men at the fort that the prisoners would soon arrive. Word was shouted from house to house:

"Osceola has been taken! They're bringing him to the fort."

The narrow, dusty streets filled rapidly with people pushing, shoving forward. Everybody wanted to see Osceola. Everybody wanted to cheer his capture. This would surely end the war!

Troops tramped into the main square and around the old slave market in the middle. Bursts of cheering fell into silence. The soldiers marched with set faces, with eyes straight forward. They didn't look proud of this capture. Osceola and his warriors stepped quietly and with dignity. A whisper swept through the throng:

"He was taken under a flag of truce. Jesup gave the orders."

"But this will end the war. Now we can go back to our plantations!"

"Well—maybe we can. Who knows?"

Through the town, over the drawbridge across the moat, and into the courtyard of the old Spanish castle walked the prisoners. They were taken to a cell, and the great door clanked shut behind them.

14

The Escape of Wildcat

Osceola sat on the floor in Fort Marion, watching his companions and saying very little. His cell was a high-ceilinged room with arched stone walls and a floor made of packed dirt. When the door opened to allow a guard to enter or leave, Osceola caught a glimpse of the open courtyard of the old fort, and of the blue sky with fluffs of cloud sailing in from the ocean. A strong salt breeze brought the cry of gull and cormorant.

Fort Marion had been Castillo San Marcos in Spanish days. At that time the drawbridge over the moat had been raised to give protection to the people of St. Augustine during attacks by pirates, Indians, or Englishmen. During the American Revolution the British, who had owned the colony, had imprisoned American patriots in its cells. When Florida became a territory of the United States, Indians were locked in Fort Marion.

On the outer wall, about eighteen feet from the floor, there was one narrow window. In the early days it had been put in the wall as a shooting hole for marksmen who stood on a stone platform beneath it. Now two iron bars were fastened in the window.

When the Seminole warriors had been locked into the cell with some of their women and children, they had not been searched for weapons until the following day. During that night Wildcat and some other warriors buried their knives in the hard dirt of the floor. Then over these places they put the straw-filled bags on which they were to sleep.

Nobody thought that any escape was possible from a fort that was like one of the strongholds of

Europe. Guards did not bother the Indians much, beyond bringing them food.

In his cell old King Philip sat sadly all day. Osceola, whose voice had roused his people to battle so many times, was gloomy and quiet.

But Wildcat and some of his followers began planning escape as soon as the locks were turned in the door. Wildcat was young, thin, and agile. He was not as brilliant a leader as Osceola, but he was quick and adventurous. He tried to urge Osceola to escape. They had been tricked and taken under a truce, Wildcat said. The war would end if the Seminoles were left without a fierce leader. Some chiefs were still free down in the Everglades, but they did not have the power of Osceola.

Wildcat went on, with one argument after another, but Osceola shook his head. From the moment that he had looked at the grim soldiers lined up behind General Hernandez, he had known that his fighting was ended. He would never submit—never agree to leave Florida. But now his powerful voice was silenced. The white men were coming in on the Indian's lands like a great roaring tidal water, sweeping everything before them. He knew that his people would have to give up their homeland. Silently he watched Wildcat prepare for escape, but Osceola would not go.

For a month Wildcat planned and waited. At night he and seventeen warriors took turns climbing up to the window to loosen the bars. This climb wasn't so difficult for Wildcat, for there was a ledge in the stone under the window.

One bar was so strongly imbedded in the stones that it could not be moved, and had to be bent slowly to one side. The other was somewhat rusty. Wildcat, whose thin hands were strong and clever, twisted and turned until, at last, he had removed the bar. However, he left it standing in place to fool the guard.

This window was five feet high but only eight inches wide. It cut through a wall that was five feet thick. The escape would be made in the dark of the moon. Five days before that time, late in November, eighteen Seminole braves and two young squaws ate as little food as possible, and took certain herbs given them by the medicine man to help them grow thin.

They removed the straw from their sleeping bags. Then they cut the bags into strips and made a rope which they hid under the straw. The young warriors fastened their knives into their belts and prepared to make the desperate attempt for freedom.

The night was dark. Scarcely a ray of light came into the cell from the little slit above. The sentinel was approaching on his rounds. Instead of opening the door, glancing in, and shutting it again, he came in, leaned against the door, and began to talk. The guard felt lonesome. A few of the Indians could speak English.

"Say," he called out, "how about a little talk? You Indians are great on talks. Let's have one now."

Silence met him. The Indians were lying on the floor, apparently sleeping.

"If you don't want to talk, how about a song?"

The guard raised his voice and started to sing.

Talmus Hadjo whispered to Wildcat, "Do you want me to leap on him? We could tie his head in a bag."

"No, we had better pretend to sleep. He will go."

The guard stopped singing. The room was silent. Not an Indian moved. The guard shrugged disgustedly. What a job, patrolling this fort! He went out, slamming the door loudly. Wildcat heard the lock turn and the guard's heavy steps growing fainter as he tramped toward the guard room. He was probably warming himself inside, and would not come out again immediately.

Wildcat and the others instantly leaped up and pulled their rope out of hiding.

One of the Indian warriors was John Cavallo, or John Horse. He was the tallest and strongest of all of the prisoners. As he placed himself on the platform below the ledge with his legs braced, Wildcat sprang to his shoulders. From there Wildcat began to climb the wall in motions as swift and

One by one the Indians escaped through the narrow prison window

silent as the savage animal of the dark forest fo
which he had been named. Reaching the ledge
the young chief raised himself to the window an
pulled out the rusty bar. He then tied one end o
the rope to the bent bar and flung the other en
down.

The Indians waited below, ears keyed to th
slightest sound from the courtyard. Would h
make it? They drew in their breath sharply an
held it, as Wildcat did.

Turning sideways and squeezing through th
narrow hole, Wildcat grasped the rope and wen
through the window head first. Suddenly he dis
appeared, and those inside heard a soft thump a
the rope tightened and he landed in the mud o
the moat.

Wildcat had left a good deal of his skin on th
sharp stones of the window opening. This did no
stop the rest of the prisoners. One after the othe
they wriggled through, including the two squaws
like wild animals escaping from a hunter's trap

The guard did not return. Overhead the moon hid, and the sky was a misty black.

Talmus Hadjo was the last man, except John Cavallo, to make his try for freedom. Hadjo was much heavier than the others. Wildcat stood below and saw the rope sway in a breeze from the ocean. Hadjo twisted and pushed. Agonizing pain swept over him as the stones scraped his flesh raw. Still he could not get through. From below Wildcat hissed, "Draw in your breath. Hard! Then push."

Talmus Hadjo took a deep breath and held it until his eyes felt as if they were popping from his head. Suddenly he shot through and fell into the moat. He landed full length, as if dead. John Cavallo descended safely and helped Wildcat lift and carry Hadjo out over the moat wall to the ground. They took him away silently to a nearby field and brought him to. As they helped him to his feet they heard a soft movement in the field. One of the Indians who had slipped over the fence had returned with a mule.

They hoisted Hadjo onto its back and moved out beyond the sleeping city to the forest. Five days later, having lived on nothing but berries and roots, they rejoined Wildcat's band on the Tomoka River.

The morning after the escape, Osceola sent a message out by the guard. He informed General Hernandez that Wildcat and nineteen others had escaped during the night—and that he, also, could have done so, but had not.

15

Strike Where You Can!

Not long after Wildcat and his group escaped from the fort in St. Augustine, Colonel Zachary Taylor landed at Tampa with a company of troops. This was the man called Old Rough and Ready, later to become a general in the Mexican war—and still later President of the United States.

Taylor found General Jesup waiting for him with an order. "Soon as you can get going, start for the Everglades."

"Just where are the hostiles, General?" asked Colonel Taylor. "Do you have any idea?"

"Nobody has," barked out Jesup, striding up

and down the room. The General was beset by troubles. Newspapers all over the country were railing at him for the way in which he had taken Osceola. Yet they were also blaming him for the escape of Wildcat. Now Wildcat and John Cavallo were starting the war again, and the General was blamed for that, too. Jesup was going to have to defend himself against public criticism for the rest of his life.

"Head for the Everglades region, Colonel Taylor," said Jesup. "Follow the Indians where you find them. Strike when and where you can! Those are the only orders I can give you."

Taylor set out with his men, joined by a force of volunteers from several states. There were over a thousand men in the command, some foot soldiers and some dragoons. On the march a few Indians were captured and sent back to Fort Mellon for safekeeping.

Taylor discovered from these prisoners that the main body of hostiles were near Lake Okeechobee

—the largest body of fresh water within the boundaries of the United States. Nobody except the Indians knew much about this region, for it had always been mysterious, unknown country.

As Taylor's advance guard approached the Everglades, three dragoons sighted a mounted Indian riding herd on cattle in a grassy prairie. One dragoon raced around to head off the escape of the Indian, while the other two charged down on him. He was captured and brought, unharmed, to the Colonel. Calling an interpreter, Taylor asked a few questions.

"Where are the main forces of Wildcat, John Cavallo, and Sam Jones?"

Silence and a sullen glance answered him.

Colonel Taylor glared at the captive from under bushy brows. "If you don't tell me, I'll hang you from that pine tree I see yonder!"

The Indian's eyes showed fear for the first time. A Seminole was afraid of no death except by hanging—for he believed that his soul could escape only through the mouth. A hanged man could not free his spirit for the Happy Hunting Grounds, and so must follow the living, doing them harm.

"They hide beyond the swamp and the saw grass, to the west," said the captive. "They wait for you."

"Ah, I see. Well," Taylor said to one of his men, "take him out and put handcuffs on him. That's one warrior who is on his way beyond the Mississippi!"

Early next day the troops were on the march. It was December 25th, and a strange Christmas Day for the men. Instead of glistening snow, they saw a dismal swamp where alligators roared at night. Instead of carols sung by children, they heard the wail of the sand-hill crane and listened for a fearful war whoop. Leaving horses and artillery at the edge of a swamp, the men crossed it and came out into a vast field of stiff saw grass growing in mud.

Taylor ordered the troops to attack. Beyond the grassy prairie was another big cypress swamp, rising gray and dark green against the sky. In these

The volunteers floundered through the stiff saw grass

trees, beneath waving curtains of moss, the desperate Indians waited with rifles cocked.

Colonel Gentry led the way with the volunteers. In his company was his son. As the men floundered through the sharp spears of grass, their feet sank in black muck. They had to hold their guns high out of the muddy water. Behind the volunteers, regulars set their teeth and waded out into the slimy prairie. The grass was as high as their necks, but it did not shelter them much, for their heads were plainly visible to the Seminole marksmen.

War whoops rang out in a wild chorus.

A hot fire of bullets plowed into the saw grass. Men went down in the mud, unable to return the fire. Some grasped their rifles firmly and picked off an Indian here or there among the swampy cypress trees. Colonel Gentry fell dead in the grass, and his son pitched over near him, seriously wounded. The volunteers, panicked by the terrible situation, turned and floundered back in the direction from which they had come. Indians whooped defiance and yelled victoriously as the men, confused and disorganized, retreated into the swamp behind them.

But the regulars came on. As fast as a head was seen above the saw grass by the Indians, it went down into the slime. Still the men came on. In one company, there was only one officer who survived this battle. Nearly all of the sergeants and corporals, and many of the men, fell. Yet those who survived advanced. As the soldiers crawled into the cypress grove, the Indians retreated, only to be pursued by the troops. Indian fought soldier in hand-to-hand combat in the dim swamp forest.

By late afternoon the Seminoles had slipped away. The troops dropped down against trees to recover enough strength to take care of their wounded and dead.

The number of wounded and dead was very great. Only ten Indian bodies were found among the wet roots of the cypress trees. But the United States forces had lost 26 dead and 112 wounded.

The army had won the Battle of Okeechobee, but at great cost. And with what result? A few Indians had been killed. The remainder had escaped once more into their watery hiding places. The war was no nearer its end than it had been before the battle. These Indians were not surrendering!

General Jesup fought an engagement not long after on the Loxahatchee River and received a face wound. Once again the Seminoles disappeared, and once again the white man was baffled. Once again the battle was called a victory for the troops. But the newspapers printed angry letters and articles about this bloody, expensive, and useless war—a war that never seemed to end, and was accomplishing little or nothing.

16

A Smile So Warm, So Strange

The authorities had no sooner heard of the escape of twenty prisoners than they ordered iron manacles placed on the ankles of the remaining warriors and chiefs. Dr. Frederick Weedon, the prison physician, stood and watched as soldiers locked iron bands on old King Philip and Osceola. Osceola looked up at the doctor with one of the flashing glances that seldom lit his dark eyes now.

"I sent word to General Jesup to tell him of the escape," said Osceola. "I could have gone—and I did not! Philip is too old to escape." He looked at the clanking chains that bound him and said scornfully, "They could not capture me except under a white flag! They cannot hold me except with a chain!"

Dr. Weedon had visited Osceola daily since his capture. The Seminole leader considered this physician his friend, and would talk to him. Dr. Weedon, who had served as a colonel in the army of Andrew Jackson during the War of 1812 and the Creek Indian War, was much interested in the Seminoles. He lived in St. Augustine and practiced medicine there, but spent more time in the fort than in his office. Dr. Weedon was my great-grandfather. Strangely enough he was also the brother-in-law of General Wiley Thompson, whose killing by Osceola started the Seminole War.

Dr. Weedon was given an opportunity to know Osceola even better when orders came to Fort Marion to ship all of the 250 Seminole prisoners to Fort Moultrie, at Charleston, South Carolina.

General Jesup knew Wildcat to be the one chief who was young, vigorous and strong enough to continue the war. All hope of a quick end to the conflict was over, and Jesup thought it better to have the Seminole prisoners placed out of the state.

Immediately they were taken aboard the steamship *Poinsett*, which was lying in the harbor. Osceola asked Dr. Weedon to go with him and the doctor agreed.

At that time, my grandfather was only a small boy. So of course he was too young to remember the day that Osceola left his own land. However, he heard the story many times from Dr. Weedon, his father, who was beside Osceola as the ship steamed out to sea.

Osceola stood at the rail and watched as the little Spanish city, gleaming in the sun under the frowning stone walls of the fort, disappeared from view. Despair was in his eyes. He would not see Florida again.

The *Poinsett* carried Osceola to Fort Moultrie,

which was built on Sullivan's Island in the harbor of Charleston. Here, certainly, no escape was possible. So the Seminole prisoners were not kept in irons, but were allowed their freedom within the prison. They had their weapons returned to them also. Osceola had with him his two wives and his two little boys.

Doctor Weedon sailed with Osceola to Fort Moultrie

By this time many stories had been printed about Osceola throughout the United States, and he had gained a reputation that was world-wide. Even the Indian tribes beyond the Rockies knew of his stern will and of his bravery. Osceola had become so famous that three artists came to Fort Moultrie to paint his portrait.

Of these the best known was George Catlin, who had lived with Indians in the East and in the West, and had painted their pictures. Osceola took a liking to the artist and often talked to him. Catlin arrived at Fort Moultrie on January 17, 1838, and began his portrait at once, the first ever to be painted of Osceola. Catlin was so interested in the remarkable young Indian leader that he wrote several descriptions of him in letters that were later published.

Dr. Weedon spoke to the artist of Osceola.

"I am much concerned about him," the doctor said. "He eats very little, and is losing weight. His health has declined since his capture. He is a young man still, only about thirty-four or -five. When I saw him first I thought him to be the finest looking man I had ever laid eyes on. I'm afraid that he does not want to live."

George Catlin looked at Osceola and nodded in agreement. He could see that the Seminole was very thin and that only his burning eyes looked alive. Yet once in a while, when something made him smile, he was like another man. Catlin wrote of him:

"I have painted him precisely in the costume in which he stood for his picture, even to a string and a trinket. He wore three ostrich feathers in his head, and a turban made of a varicolored cotton shawl—and his dress was chiefly of calicos, with a handsome bead sash or belt around his waist and his rifle in his hand.

"This young man is, no doubt, an extraordinary character, as he has been for some years reputed, and doubtless looked upon by the Seminoles as the master spirit and leader of the tribe, although he is not a chief. From his boyhood he had led an energetic and desperate sort of life——

"During the time I have been here I have occupied a large room in the officers' quarters, by the politeness of Captain Morrison, who has command of the post, and charge of the prisoners; and on every evening, after painting all day at their portraits, I have had Osceola, Michenopah, Cloud, Coahadjo, King Philip and others in my room, until a late hour at night, where they have taken great pains to give me an account of the war, and the mode in which they were captured, of which they complain bitterly."

Catlin also wrote that Osceola was a man of medium height, with an elastic and graceful movement when he walked. His face was sad and usually gloomy, but his smile was so warm and of so strange a kind that "The world may be ransacked all over without finding another just like it. In his manners in company he is polite and gentlemanly, though all his conversation is in his own tongue;

"I'm afraid that he does not want to live"

and his general appearance and actions, those of a full-blooded and wild Indian."

Sometimes Osceola sat sadly, his eyes like deep dark pools of water in the dim swamps. Then Dr. Weedon talked to him cheerfully and hopefully of the West and his future home there. Often there was no response, and the doctor knew that Osceola believed he would never see the West. Once, however, Osceola was in a more cheerful mood than usual. He talked of the many battles and skirmishes of the past several years. Then he rose and began to imitate the soldiers.

First he showed how the white men fought, loading and firing. Then he showed how the Indian fought. Laughing, he said to the doctor, "I wore this plume when I defeated General Gaines, these spurs when I drove back General Clinch, and these moccasins when I whipped General Call!"

On the doctor's next visit, he tried to persuade Osceola to take a tonic to improve his appetite. In a friendly way, the Seminole war leader held out an ornament that he often wore. It was a round piece of silver, made from a thinly beaten silver dollar and decorated with punched holes. The doctor looked at the ornament.

"You wish to give it to me? I am very grateful."

Osceola's rare warm smile broke across his drawn face. He handed Dr. Weedon his small brass pipe bowl, engraved with palm leaves.

"Take this, too," he urged the doctor. "You have helped me. You have been my only white friend."

As the doctor left the room he shook his head. There was something so final about the giving of these things—as if Osceola felt that he would not need them any more.

17

Farewell!

Dr. Weedon was awakened one cold night late in January by a tapping on his door. At first he thought that he had been dreaming—then the tapping came again. He got up and shivered as he opened the door. It was the Indian interpreter.

"Doctor, come to Osceola. He is very sick!"

"Tell him I'll be there in a few minutes."

When the doctor entered the room he saw Osceola lying on his blankets on the floor, before a flickering fire in the fireplace. Beyond him sat his two wives and the two children, watching silently.

Dr. Weedon knelt beside the sick man and felt his pulse. It was quick and hard, and indicated high fever. Then he examined the patient's face and neck. Osceola's breathing was rapid and very difficult, and his expression showed that he was in great pain. The doctor looked into his throat. The tonsils were much enlarged and inflamed. He had a disease called quinsy.

As Dr. Weedon got to his feet he called for his medical bag. Two officers of the fort had been summoned also, and were standing near by. At this moment an Indian medicine man called a prophet came softly into the room and stared down at Osceola, who fixed his eyes on him.

When Dr. Weedon brought medicine to the patient, Osceola shook his head in refusing. From that moment he would not allow the doctor to treat him.

Next morning Dr. Weedon got into a boat and went ashore. He went directly to Dr. B. B. Strobel, who was professor of anatomy at Charleston Medical College, and asked for assistance. Perhaps a strange doctor might succeed where he had failed.

Twilight was drawing in early across the water, creeping into the dark room of the fort, throwing strange shadows on the figure of Osceola. Except for the harsh breath of the sick man, there was no sound as the two doctors entered.

Two soldiers brought in candles and placed them on the floor beside Osceola. He was lying on his blanket on the floor, before the flickering fire, his head propped up. His two wives knelt at either side, bathing his neck with warm water in which some odorous herbs had been steeped.

"Osceola," Dr. Strobel began, "will you let me look at your throat?"

The sick man nodded, and the doctor saw with dismay that there was danger of suffocation from the swelling.

"Will you let me scarify the tonsils?" Dr. Strobel asked.

Osceola fixed his eyes on the conjurer, or medicine man, who sat near by. He was wrapped to the chin in his blanket and had all the dignity of a great man. The interpreter repeated the question.

The conjurer whipped out, "No!"

The two doctors stared at each other, and then Dr. Strobel begged, "Osceola, your life is in danger. Will you let me apply leeches to draw blood from your neck? Or give you medicine?"

The conjurer, on hearing the question, snapped, "No!"

The physicians stayed for a long time and then, completely baffled and helpless, they had to leave Osceola to his fate.

George Catlin, who had finished his portrait of Osceola on January 25th, stayed on a few days longer. He often went to sit with the sick man and talk to him for a little while through the interpreter. Osceola could not speak, but when, on January 29th, the artist came to tell him good-bye, the Seminole smiled and gave him a warm hand shake.

As Catlin went on board ship for his voyage

back to Philadelphia, he thought of the many chieftains of many tribes he had painted. He recalled the Indians of the far-off western plains and mountains, and he felt that never had he painted a finer looking or more courageous Indian than Osceola.

On January 30th, Dr. Weedon saw that his patient was failing. Osceola seemed to know it too, for he asked, by signs, to have the chiefs and the officers of the post brought in. He made signs to his two wives and his children to bring him his full dress. With astonishing strength he sat up, put on his long shirt, his leggings and his moccasins. Then he girded on his war-belt, hung his bullet pouch and powderhorn over his shoulder, and laid his knife down by his side on the floor.

Osceola motioned toward his red paint and his looking glass, which was held up before him. Slowly he painted one-half of his face, his neck, and his throat with vermilion. Then he painted the backs of his hands, his wrists, and the handle of his knife red. This was a ceremony that came when the Indians took an oath of war and destruction.

He then placed his knife in its sheath under his belt. Next, he reached up to arrange most carefully the three ostrich plumes in the back of his turban, which he had wound about his head.

Sinking back slowly on his blanket, as his people and the officers and the doctor stood silently about him, Osceola lay down to gain a little strength. Then he sat up again, and with a brilliant, friendly smile, extended his hand to Dr. Weedon, to all of the officers and chiefs, and to his wives and children. There was no sound in the dim room but the embers dropping in the fireplace.

Osceola raised his hand and with a graceful movement made a sign to be lowered to his blanket. He slowly drew from his war-belt his scalping knife, and, grasping it firmly in his right hand, laid it across his other hand on his breast. A moment later he smiled away his last breath, without a struggle or a groan.

Osceola made a sign to be lowered to his blanket

Osceola was buried with full military honors. He had an escort of two doctors, the Seminole Indians, who were led by the chiefs, the officers of the army post, and a detachment of troops. Boats came over from Charleston all day in a choppy sea, carrying people who wished to attend the funeral of Osceola. A large group stood by in a cold salt wind, with heads bowed, as the troops fired a last salute over the grave of a brave and valiant warrior.

The grave of Osceola is on Sullivan's Island, near the fort where he died, with a stone shaft erected near by. On the shaft is this inscription:

OSCEOLA

Patriot and Warrior

Died at Fort Moultrie

January 30th, 1838

During the following month all of the Seminole captives were put aboard ship under the guardianship of Captain Morrison, and taken to the western

Indian territory. Old King Philip, however, did not outlive Osceola long, for he died on the way west. His son, Wildcat, was again leading the Seminoles in Florida in the war that flamed up once more like a fire in wild grasses.

18

The Play Must Go On

No matter how many Seminoles surrendered, there were others who would never give in. Every chief of every little band made his own decision. Micanopy was supposed to be the head chief, yet even when he said to the army officers, "I have my face turned to the West, and will go with all my people," not many followed him.

Jumper took his little band along, and they sailed from Tampa Bay, for Jumper was ill of tuberculosis and no longer willing to fight. Down in the deep Everglades, however, the chief called Arpeika —known to the white people as Sam Jones—said hat he had never signed a treaty and would never eave.

In the spring of 1838 General Jesup was transerred, and Zachary Taylor became commanding eneral. General Alexander Macomb came down rom Washington and called a meeting of several hiefs at Fort King. The Indians desperately vanted peace, and asked only that they might be llowed to remain deep in the marshes of the Everlades, where no white man wished to live. General Macomb did not ask them to sign an agreement, nd he gave them no guarantees, but he told them hat they could stay in the Everglades.

The bands had no sooner gone south again than he people of Florida and Georgia set up an uproar in the newspapers and cried out everywhere hat the Indians must go or be wiped out completely. Now the Indians knew that the truce neant nothing—and once again they went on the varpath.

An island called Indian Key was attacked by var canoes filled with Indians in war paint. They killed Dr. Perrine, a noted scientist who had brought seeds from Yucatan to Florida to start the growing of useful tropical plants.

Lieutenant-Colonel Harney and twenty-six dragoons set out for the Caloosahatchee River with a heavy load of supplies. They were going to Florida's west coast to set up a trading post for the Indians, who had seemed very friendly. When Harney's men reached the mouth of the river, they made camp without posting a sentinel and went to sleep under their mosquito nets on the shore of the Gulf of Mexico.

Just before dawn they were shocked awake by wild war whoops of Indians, who leaped on the tents and dragged the men out, killing and scalping them. Some of the soldiers got away and ran for the woods. Harney and two others jumped into a canoe and pushed off from shore. Others swam out to a vessel lying at anchor in the harbor. Thirteen men were slain, and the Indians got away with the supplies, including rifles and ammunition. Harney was fighting mad. He swore that he would hunt down Seminoles until they were all removed or dead.

Bloodhounds were brought from Cuba to track the Indians, but failed. Foot soldiers, sailors, marines, and dragoons all joined in the war. Now they were led on expeditions by Harney, who did not stop at sloughs, saw grass, swamps, or rivers. Boats were made of hard cypress, in the Mackinac fashion that men used on the Great Lakes. In them troops rowed up rivers and across lakes, always searching for Indians.

Rough and Ready Commander Zachary Taylor—and then, later on, General Armistead—sent out one party of troops after another. The men from all the armed services lived together and fought together as one group—in mud, rain, and under burning sun. They killed snakes, fought mosquitoes, and lived in wet clothes, eating cold food fairly often.

Here and there they found Indian houses on islands deep in the swamps and Everglades prairies. These they destroyed. Once in a while they cap-

The Indians plundered the wagon of stage costumes

tured women and children, and sent them to For
Mellon. When they caught an armed warrio
they sometimes hanged him from a tree.

Still the war went on. Farther north Wildca
ambushed a theatrical troupe jolting along the roa
in a carriage and a wagon from Picolata to St
Augustine. This was the company of W. C
Forbes of Savannah, Georgia. Two traveler
named Vose and Miller had joined the troupe.

As they rattled into the eleven-mile zone aroun
St. Augustine protected by the military, they fel
safe. They began to smile and talk of the shrimp

nd-rice dinner they expected to get in a short ime in the city.

Suddenly a war whoop rang on their ears from dense thicket of palmetto. Shaking all over, the nen leaped to the ground and ran in all directions. A German musician was shot as he tried to hide behind the carriage. Vose and Miller were wounded, but dashed to the woods.

Led by Wildcat, twenty Indians in war paint sprang out into the road. One of the actors dodged nto the waters of a small swamp near by, but the Indians did not look for him or for the others who had escaped. They were too interested in plundering the wagon of stage costumes to pay any attention to their victims.

Seven dragoons, hearing shots, came racing up the road on their horses. The Seminoles, grabbing as many costumes as they could carry, fled into the woods. As the troops examined the musician, who was lying dead in the road, all the others came staggering back except one actor. They finally found him up to the neck in swamp water, with his head hidden under a big leaf of the bonnet plant.

Woefully the players arrived in St. Augustine. But a show must go on! That night, without a musician, they put on their play with make-shift costumes. It was called *The Honeymoon*, and never had the actors played to such a crowded house, or received such wild applause!

19

Wildcat Goes West

Wildcat and his fierce band roamed the woods and swamps. They were not caught, but after a time Colonel Worth's troops brought in a girl who said that she was Wildcat's daughter. At the direction of Colonel Worth, the girl sent word to her father, asking him to come in to claim her.

When Wildcat and his warriors arrived in answer to the message, the Colonel and his officers were almost too surprised to greet them. The Indians were dressed in costumes that had been taken from the company of actors! Some of the Seminoles wore Roman togas, like Julius Caesar. Some had on helmets, and some plumed hats. Wildcat was clothed in the black velvet doublet and hose of Hamlet, surmounted—with dignity—by the bright turban and waving feathers of a Seminole chief.

Wildcat promised Colonel Worth that if he could have his daughter he would bring in his people to be sent west. While Wildcat was getting his tribesmen together, however, there took place one of those upsetting mistakes that occurred over and over in the Seminole War.

Major Childs, not knowing of Colonel Worth's promise, captured Wildcat, his brother, his uncle, and thirteen other warriors. All of them were immediately shipped to New Orleans. As soon as Colonel Worth heard of this he got in touch with the War Department in Washington, and demanded that Wildcat be returned to Tampa.

So Wildcat and his warriors were amazed when their ship, which had been lying in harbor at New

Orleans, turned around for a return voyage to Florida. In due time, Colonel Worth received word that the vessel was lying in Tampa Bay, but he sent orders out to the captain to remain at anchor two miles off shore. Then he boarded a launch and went out to the transport.

The Colonel stood grimly on deck and waited for the prisoners to be brought up to him. He would see to it that this chief, who was the most respected leader since the death of Osceola, surrendered his entire band.

Morning sun glittered on the bay as a salty breeze swept landward to cool the summer day. Near the transport, a pelican dove for fish and came up to raise his great beak high to let the food slide into his pouch. Closer to shore a government schooner and several other vessels rode the swells.

As the Indians came upon deck there was no sound from the crew or from the soldiers who stood stiffly behind their colonel. But the iron shackles on the wrists and ankles of the warriors clattered and clanked. The chains were so heavy that the downcast Indians could move their feet only a few inches at a time. They came forward and ranged themselves before the soldiers according to their rank as warriors. Their heads drooped, and their eyes were fixed on the planking of the deck.

Colonel Worth addressed Wildcat, using his Indian name, "Coacoochee." As the officer began to talk his voice held a friendly tone, but before he finished, it rang out with the deadly menace of a volley of rifle shots.

"Coacoochee, I take you by the hand as a warrior, a brave man!" said the Colonel. "You have fought long and with a true and strong heart for your country. I take your hand with pride. But you have raised the war whoop again and again. Many times you and your warriors have stained the earth with the blood of the white man and of his wife and children. This war must end! You are the man to end it. I wish you to say how many days are needed to talk to your people.

"You can select three or five of these warriors to bring in your people," Colonel Worth went on. "I wish your relatives and friends told this. Unless they do as you tell them, you and your warriors here will be hanged from the yard arm of this vessel, when the sun sets on the day appointed—with the irons on your hands and feet!"

Wildcat and his warriors raised their heads and stared at the Colonel's grim face with searching looks. When Wildcat spoke his voice was low and his eyes, and those of his fighting men, were hopeless.

"I was once a boy, hunting in the forests, first with the bow and arrow, and then with the rifle. I saw the white man, far off, and I was told that he was my enemy. I could not shoot him as I would a wolf or a bear. Yet, like those enemies, he came upon me. Horses and cattle and fields he took from me. He said that he was my friend! Then he abused our women and children and told us to go from our own land.

"He gave us his hand in friendship. We took it

—while taking it, we found that in the other hand he held a snake. His tongue was forked like the snake's. I asked but a small piece of land, enough to plant and live, far to the south—a spot in which to lay the ashes of my wife and child some day. This was not granted to me. I wish now to go ashore, without the irons on my hands and feet, and talk to my people."

Colonel Worth shook his head. "This war must end," he insisted. "You will not be allowed to go ashore without the irons. You can only send some of your warriors to speak to your people."

Wildcat chose five warriors to take his message. Then he asked for forty sticks. Thirty-nine of them he gave to his messengers, saying sadly, "Tell my people that they must all come to Fort Brooke, to go across the water with me. Each stick is for one day." Then he took his scalping knife, made a small cut on his arm, and smeared the blood on the last stick. "This is for the fortieth day. If they are not here their chief will be hanged."

Wildcat slowly drew a handkerchief from his

belt, and took a silver pin from his scarf. These he handed to one of the messengers, saying, "Give these to my wife and my daughter."

At this moment the guns of the government vessel boomed out across the water.

"What was that for?" asked Wildcat.

The crew of the transport said nothing, and the soldiers frowned. Colonel Worth bit his lip and turned on his heel, leaving the question unanswered. Nobody wanted to tell the captive Indians that this day was the Fourth of July, and that the guns were saluting Independence Day for the white man.

The messengers were taken ashore without their shackles and allowed to go free. For a month the transport rode at anchor in the bay, with Wildcat and his warriors sitting silently on deck, waiting. A lieutenant came out at the end of a week, and Wildcat smiled for the first time as he heard the message. One group of his people had come in. A few days later more appeared, and then others.

When, on the fortieth day, the chief was told

For a month Wildcat sat on deck, waiting

that his entire band of seventy-eight men, sixty-four women, and forty-seven children were encamped near Fort Brooke, his head went up proudly. Once more he looked like Wildcat, son of King Philip, as he said:

"Now take off my iron chains, that I may meet my warriors like a man!"

Colonel Worth granted him this and allowed

him to go ashore under guard. As Wildcat set foot on shore he raised both arms over his head and gave a shrill whoop. At Fort Brooke, dressed in scarlet and green, with his red turban and nodding plumes on his head, the chief spoke to his band.

"You have listened to my words and obeyed them," he said. "I thank you. The rifle is now hidden, and the white man and the red man are friends."

He was permitted to remain on shore with his people as members of other bands joined them. The time passed as pleasantly as possible, for the Indians held ball games and were given food and clothing. Then the transports took them on board and sailed for the West.

Alligator and John Cavallo had gone to the new territory earlier. Now Wildcat and his band joined them. But the territory was bad for the Seminoles. They had to live with the Creeks whom they hated, and the government never gave the tribes from Florida enough food or tools, cattle or clothing. So John Cavallo and Wildcat led a little band of Indians down into Mexico, where they lived for many years. There Wildcat died of smallpox in 1859.

20

Feet in Sand—Face to the Sun

The Seminole War was over! So they said up in Washington in 1842. And it was–in a way. Troops were withdrawn, and in 1845 Florida became a state. Altogether 11,702 Indians had been sent west from Florida, and 4,000 of them died on the way.

The war with the Seminoles was longer, more expensive, and more destructive to life than any other Indian war in the history of the United States. It had cost the government $40,000,000. During the fighting, 3,000 soldiers, sailors, and marines had died from wounds and disease, and many white settlers had lost their lives and property.

In the Seminole wars, more than a dozen generals received training that stood them well in Mexico, in California, and on the Great Plains. Two of the generals—Andrew Jackson and Zachary Taylor—became presidents. Many of the officers who had been young during the Florida war fought on different sides during the Civil War, twenty years later.

Yet 150 Indians remained in Florida, deep in the lost lands of the wet southernmost prairies. In the 1850's Billy Boleck—Bowlegs, as he was called—and a small band of warriors went on the warpath again to avenge the looting and burning of their homes by renegade white men. Billy Bowlegs eventually went west, but not all of the Seminoles did. After that they were left alone in their Florida homes.

They are still there. As Florida grew during the 1900's, stagecoaches and river steamers were followed by railroads. Great groves of oranges and grapefruit produced fruit for the markets. Cattle ranches spread out across the prairies where dragoons had fired at lurking Indian warriors. Tourists came down to enjoy the warm sun of winter and the tropical land. Towns and cities sprang up where Seminole villages had stood with their palm-thatched chikees almost invisible among the palmettos.

The Seminoles went on living as they always had

Yet the Seminoles lived as they always had, with their own laws, customs, and habits. They poled their cypress canoes among islands in the deep glades, where their chikees stood. They hunted and fished. They knew how to get along with big-jawed alligators and deadly snakes. They watched the blue heron, the white egret, and the rosy flamingo build their nests. When the pollen of the saw grass hung low and strange on the horizon, the Seminoles knew that a hurricane was coming. Then they hurriedly moved to higher ground.

In the 1860's a sewing-machine salesman penetrated the glades and sold little hand-cranked machines to the Seminole women. On these the Indians learned to make brilliant skirts, blouses, and shirts of thousands of tiny pieces of calico, sewed together with remarkable skill.

In 1938 the government set aside reservations for the Seminole tribes—for there are still two groups, quite different in language. They are called the Cow Creek and the Big Cypress tribes.

The Cow Creek band now lives farther north, west of Lake Okeechobee, on dry land, and it has become a cattle ranching tribe.

The Big Cypress group is in the watery country, where the Indians hunt and fish from canoes, and sell curios by the roadsides. They live with the tropical birds of the Everglades—egrets, herons, white ibis, and great bald eagles. They also kill deer, panther, wildcat, and bear, as well as squirrel, opossum, and rabbit.

The Seminoles in Florida have never signed a treaty of surrender to the United States government. So, unlike other Indians, they are not given government money. They work for what they get. But the government is providing schools, hospitals, and agricultural aids for them. There are more than 500 Seminoles in Florida now. Some of them live away from the reservations, working at different jobs or at farming.

Throughout the United States, you will often come upon the name "Osceola." It might be the name of a town, a county, a product, or even a man's first name! In Florida the name Osceola is frequently met in lakes, streets, people and places—and a naval vessel has borne the name.

Osceola is not forgotten by his people, in the land that he called his own. He was not born in Florida—and he did not die in Florida. His bones lie in South Carolina. Although the fate of his two children who were taken west is not known, many of the Seminoles dwelling in the glades are his family descendants. They bear the name Osceola. Stories, legends, and songs cling to his name as closely as gray moss clings to the branches of a giant live oak.

Not long ago two Seminole men who had received some extra money for alligator skins came to see New York. They got off the train in midwinter, and walked out of Pennsylvania Station to the street. There the freezing air struck through their bright striped cotton shirts and thin trousers. They stared at the tall buildings for a moment, muttered to each other—and walked back inside.

The startled agent sold them return tickets, and they got on the next train for south Florida.

Seminoles live in Florida. Their feet walk in sand, and their faces know the salt wind and the hot tropical sun. Seminoles like Florida. They intend to stay there. And they are the only Indians who have never signed a treaty of surrender to the government of the United States.

Index